RUDOLF STEINER
IN THE WALDORF SCHOOL

[VI]

FOUNDATIONS OF WALDORF EDUCATION

Rudolf Steiner
in the
Waldorf School

Lectures and Addresses
to Children, Parents, and Teachers

1919 – 1924

Translated by Catherine E. Creeger

Ⓔ Anthroposophic Press

The publisher wishes to acknowledge the inspiration
and support of Connie and Robert Dulaney

❖ ❖ ❖

This book is a translation of *Rudolf Steiner in der Waldorfschule: Ansprachen für Kinder, Eltern und Lehrer* (volume 298 in the Collected Works) published by Rudolf Steiner Verlag, Dornach, Switzerland, 1980.

© Copyright Anthroposophic Press, 1996

Published in the United States by Anthroposophic Press
RR 4 Box 94-A1, Hudson, NY 12534

LIBRARY OF CONGRESS CATALOGING-IN-PUBLICATION DATA

Steiner, Rudolf, 1861–1925.
  [Rudolf Steiner in der Waldorfschule. English]
  Rudolf Steiner in the Waldorf School : lectures and addresses
to children, parents, and teachers. 1919–1924 / translated by
Catherine E. Creeger.
    p. cm. — (Foundations of Waldorf education : 6)
  Includes bibliographical references (p. 228) and index.
  ISBN 0-88010-433-3
  1. Waldorf method of education. 2. Anthroposophy. I. Title.
II. Series
LB1029.W34S73713 1996
371.3'9—dc20   95-51541
                                                                CIP

10 9 8 7 6 5 4 3 2 1

CONTENTS

It is December 21, 1919, and Rudolf Steiner is addressing a Christmas assembly of teachers, parents, and students of the newly formed Waldorf School. "Do you love your teachers?" he asks the children. "Yes," comes the resounding reply. A few minutes later in his talk he repeats, ". . . I would like to ask you again, 'Don't you all sincerely love your teachers?'" "Yes, we do," shout the children. These earnest questions and fervent answers are repeated many times in the next few years on his frequent visits to the school.

Many who were present on such occasions have described how Steiner would make his way across the school grounds besieged by a sea of children clinging to his coat and trousers. How many Waldorf teachers today, while seeking insight into a pedagogical problem, planning a parent meeting, or preparing a public presentation wish to have before them this founder of the education! How many dream of having Rudolf Steiner present on their campuses to provide inspiration and direction!

In these addresses English-speaking readers can share a bit of the enthusiasm felt by those who experienced the presence of this remarkable Austrian philosopher and spiritual scientist. All of the talks in this collection were given between September 1919 and June 1924 at the first Waldorf School in Stuttgart, Germany. The addresses to students, teachers, and parents were offered on such occasions as the opening of the school year, Christmas and Easter assemblies, parents meetings, and the opening of a new building. One particularly poignant talk was delivered immediately following the tragic burning of the Goetheanum, the newly constructed center of the anthroposophical movement inaugurated by Steiner. Other lectures were delivered to the Waldorf School Association, which had been founded on May 19, 1920. Guided by such executive committee members as Emil Molt, Karl Stockmeyer, and Steiner himself, along with honorary chair Max Marx from the Waldorf Astoria Cigarette factory, the association had the tasks of financing the school and disseminating the ideas of Waldorf education.

Steiner's words to the students are warm, admonishing, and imaginative. His direct references to matters of the spirit are particularly thought-provoking and might surprise some modern readers. For example, he mentions "... the divine spirit that watches over your souls from the time you go to sleep until the time you wake up. ..." He tells the children that the source of their teachers' strength and ability is the Christ. He also speaks of the spirit of the Waldorf School, identifying it directly as "... the spirit of Christianity that wafts through all our rooms. ..." In June of 1921 he advises pupils that they must prepare themselves for work not only in this world, but also for that world in which they will live as spirit.

These references may mystify today's readers who will also find Steiner's assurance to parents that anthroposophy will not be directly taught in the schools: the relationship with the spirit is a matter for the individual, to be pursued in a climate of freedom. He clarifies that anthroposophy does not have to do with "what" is being taught, but with "how" it is being taught out of a "... profound and loving understanding of the human being." American readers, accustomed to keeping matters of church and state very separate, may find these lectures to be challenging. Do the above passages concerning Christ and the spirit reveal something that is of the essence of Waldorf education, or are they merely reflecting the context of time and place? In 1920, references to Christianity would not have been unusual even in American public schools, and certainly the family make-up of the first Waldorf School was predominately

Christian. On the other hand, a rightly understood regard for
Christ as the leading spirit or archetype of humanity is important for anthroposophists today. Continuing dialogue, first
among Waldorf educators and then with parents, can provide
the discrimination necessary to address these questions of freedom and spirituality.

Another major theme is the contribution of a rightly conceived education to the renewal of social life. Steiner laments
over the "…human wrecks serving in responsible positions,"
and on "… those brutal and violent human beings who come
out trampling everything under their feet as a consequence of
not having been able to cultivate their will." Later he declares,
"Social issues are not resolved in the way we often imagine
today. They are resolved by putting the right people into public
life, and this will only happen if people are able to grow up really
healthy in body and soul."

Steiner warns against the tendency for schools to become
denominational, or to serve only particular economic groups
and political interests. Such trends only take us further from
the universally human aspect of education and promote a
bureaucratic character in teaching. Cautioning that by nature a
teacher can never be a civil servant, and that education must be
an affair of the free cultural life, independent of the state, at the
same time he declares that "… we must do everything we can
to make the idea of the Waldorf School and all its impulses
become ever more popular, so that people begin to see it as a
challenge of our times."

The numerous Waldorf schools in Germany may have had
some hope of carrying this mandate to influence social life, but
in America there were only ten schools as late as 1965. In the last
twenty years, however, a change has taken place and there are
now over one hundred twenty schools and several public Waldorf teacher training colleges, university education departments,

and state and local departments of education. The increased visibility of Waldorf education has prompted questions about its role in wider educational reform. As the Sacramento Unified School District begins a public Waldorf-inspired magnet school financed by a federal grant, the superintendent responsible for initiating this collaboration with Waldorf education assumes his duties as chancellor of the New York City schools, arguably one of the most important posts of its kind in America. The impact of such contacts on public policy, educational planning, and the Waldorf movement itself remains to be seen.

Much of the time and effort that could have been devoted to movement-wide response to the above challenges, has been spent in trying to solve the monetary difficulties inherent in a privately financed education. Many teachers and boards of trustees attempt a variety of solutions aimed at both securing a quality education and adequately supporting faculty and staff. It will be encouraging to some that Steiner speaks directly to this problem of money and our attitudes toward it. He derides those who declare, "I am an idealist, I despise my wallet. I do not want to get my fingers dirty; I am much too great an idealist for that!" Later he mentions, "And since teachers cannot live on air, this requires the means to support them."

Steiner addresses a wide range of topics in this volume. He includes such subjects as the role of the parents in the schools, the economic life of the school, the social mission of Waldorf education and its relationship to the school reform movement. However, if the reader expects to find easy prescriptions for the tasks of the present time, there may be disappointment. I suspect that the true value of these talks lies in the questions they prompt, in the issues they raise. Particularly from this perspective, they are a welcome addition to the national dialogue on school reform, providing insight to Waldof and public educators alike as we grapple with these vital concerns.

1 9 1 9

The Pedagogical Basis of the Waldorf School [1]

A n   E s s a y

The intentions that Emil Molt hopes to realize through the Waldorf School relate to very specific views on our social tasks at present and in the near future.[2] The spirit in which this school is to be led must arise from these views. This school is associated with an industrial enterprise, and the way in which modern industry has taken its place in the evolution of human life and society has left its stamp on the practices of the contemporary social movement. The parents entrusting their children to this school can only hope and expect that these children will be educated to become competent in life in a sense that takes this social movement fully into account. This makes it necessary for us in founding this school to take our start from pedagogical principles that are rooted in what life in the present demands of

---

1. This essay was written for the *Waldorf-Nachrichten* [Waldorf News]), Stuttgart, No. 19, October 1919. It can now be found in *Aufsätze über die Dreigliederung des sozialen Organismus und zur Zeitlage 1915-1921* [Essays on Threefolding the Social Organism and on the Situation of the Times, 1915–1921], pp. 83ff, GA 24, Dornach, 1961, and in a special edition, *Die pädagogishe Grundlage und Zielsetzung der Waldorfschule*, [The Pedagogical Basis of the Waldorf School and Establishing its Goals], three essays, Dornach, 1978.
2. Emil Molt, 1876-1936, was the owner of the Waldorf-Astoria cigarette factory. In this capacity he founded the Waldorf School, which was intended at its inception for the children of the blue and white-collar workers of his factory. He asked Rudolf Steiner to take on the organization and leadership of the school.

us. Our children are to be educated to become people who are prepared for a life that corresponds to these demands, which are ones that anyone can support, regardless of what social class he or she comes from. What real present-day life demands of people must be reflected in the organization of this school. The spirit that is to govern this life must be stimulated in the children through how they are taught.

It would be disastrous if a spirit foreign to life were to prevail in the basic pedagogical views on which the Waldorf School is to be founded. Such a spirit appears all too easily nowadays wherever we develop a feeling for the part that our immersion in a materialistic attitude and way of life in recent decades has played in the breakdown of our civilization. This feeling leads to the desire to introduce an idealistic attitude into our administration of public affairs, and anyone who has been paying attention to the development of our educational system will want to see this attitude realized there more than anywhere else. Naturally, we must acknowledge the great deal of good will that is expressed in this way of looking at things. If it becomes active in the right way, it will be of great service in rallying human forces for a social undertaking for which new prerequisites must be created. And yet, in just such a case it is necessary to point out that even the best will must fail if it sets out to turn intentions into realities without fully taking into account the prerequisites that are based on insight into the matter.

This characterizes one of the challenges that must be taken into consideration nowadays in founding institutions such as the Waldorf School is intended to be. Idealism must be at work within the spirit of its pedagogy and methods, but this must be an idealism that has the power to awaken in growing human beings those forces and abilities that they will need for the rest of their lives in order to work competently for their community of contemporaries and to have a livelihood that will sustain them.

Educational theory and methodology will be able to meet this challenge only if they possess a real understanding of the growing human being. Nowadays people of insight are demanding an education that aims not at one-sided knowledge, but at the ability to do things, not at merely cultivating intellectual gifts but at training the will. This idea is undoubtedly correct. However, it is not possible to educate the will and the healthy soul that underlies it unless we develop insights that awaken energetic impulses in the soul and will. A frequent mistake nowadays in this regard consists not in presenting the growing human being with an excess of insight, but in cultivating insights that lack impact as far as life is concerned. Anyone who believes that it is possible to educate the will without cultivating the insight that enlivens it is succumbing to illusion. Clear-sightedness on this point is a task for present-day pedagogy, but it can come only from a life-filled understanding of the whole human being.

As it is imagined for the time being, the Waldorf School will be a primary school that teaches its students through basing its educational goals and curriculum on insight into the nature of the total human being, an insight that must be alive in each teacher to the extent that this is already possible under current circumstances. Naturally, the children in each grade must be brought to the point where they can meet demands that are made in accordance with contemporary ways of looking at things. Within this framework, however, the shape that all instructional goals and curricula take must result from the above-characterized understanding of the human being and of life.

Children are entrusted to primary school in a period of life in which their soul-constitution is undergoing a significant transformation. Between birth and the sixth or seventh year of life, with regard to everything that is to be educated in them, human beings are predisposed to give themselves over completely to what is closest in their human surroundings and to use their instinct for imitation to shape their own emerging forces. After this point, their souls are open to consciously receiving what works on them from teachers or educators on the basis of a natural, unquestioned authority. Children accept this authority out of the dim feeling that there is something that lives in their teachers and educators that should also live in them. You cannot be an educator or a teacher without relating to children with full insight. Their urge to imitate has been transformed into a receptivity based on a natural and uncontested relationship of authority, and you must take this into account in the broadest possible sense.

Contemporary humanity's way of looking at life, based as it is on mere insight into nature, does not approach such phenomena of human development with full consciousness. Only those with a sense for a human being's most subtle expressions of life can devote the necessary attention to these phenomena. Such a sense must prevail in the art of teaching. It must shape the curriculum; it must be alive in the spirit that unites teacher and student.

What teachers do can depend to only a slight extent on what the general standards of abstract educational theory stimulate in them. It must rather be born anew, in each moment of their activity, out of their living understanding of the developing human being. Naturally, the objection can be raised that life-filled teaching of this sort will fail because of classes with a large number of students. Within certain limits, this objection is certainly justified. However, those who take it beyond these limits only demonstrate that they are speaking from the viewpoint of an abstract, normative theory of education. In fact, a living art of teaching, one that rests on a true understanding of the human being, has a thread of strength running through it that stimulates individual students to participate, so that it is not necessary to keep their attention through direct "individualized" treatment. It is possible to structure the subject that is being dealt with so that each student learns and grasps it in an individual way. For this to happen, what the teacher is doing need only be sufficiently strongly alive. For those who have a sense for a true understanding of the human being, the developing human being becomes one of life's riddles to solve, to such an extent that their attempt at solving it rouses their students to participate. Participation of this sort is more fruitful than individualized treatment, which all too easily paralyzes the student as far as real independent activity is concerned. Still staying within certain limits, it may be stated that larger classes with teachers who are full of the life that is stimulated by a true understanding of the human being will achieve greater success than small classes with teachers who are incapable of this because they take a normative theory of education as their starting point.

A keen understanding of the human being will discover another transformation in soul-constitution that takes place around the end of the ninth year. This is less pronounced than the transformation in the sixth or seventh year, but just as significant for the art of teaching. Around age nine, children's feeling of ego identity assumes a form that makes it more possible to speak to them about the relationships of things and processes among themselves, whereas earlier the interest they developed was almost exclusively in the relationship of things and processes to human beings. Such phenomena of human development must be taken into account very carefully by teachers and educators. When what we introduce into the children's world of ideas and feelings is in line with the direction of the developmental forces of a given stage of life, we strengthen the entire developing person in a way that remains a source of strength throughout that person's life. If we work counter to the direction of development at any given stage, however, we weaken the person.

The basis for developing an appropriate curriculum lies in recognizing the specific challenges of different stages of life. This also forms the basis for how subject matter is treated in successive stages. By the end of the children's ninth year, we will need to have brought them to a certain level in everything that has streamed into human life through the evolution of culture. Therefore, we are right in spending the first few school years in teaching writing and reading, but we must arrange this instruction in a way that does justice to the nature of child development in this stage of life. If our teaching one-sidedly takes advantage of the children's intellect and abstractly acquired abilities, their willing and feeling nature will be stunted. In contrast, if the children learn in a way that allows the whole human being to take part in the activity, they will develop in a well-rounded way. When children draw or do rudimentary painting, the whole human being develops an interest in what is being done. This is why we should allow writing to develop from drawing. We should derive the forms of the letters from shapes that allow the child's naive artistic sense to make itself felt. We should develop writing, which guides us toward the element of meaning and intellect, out of an activity that is artistic and attracts the interest of the whole human being. Reading, which draws our attention very strongly into the intellectual realm, should be allowed to develop only as a result of writing.

Once we realize how much can be gained intellectually from a naive artistic education, we will tend to grant art its fair place in early elementary education. We will incorporate the musical and graphic arts appropriately into the classroom and link physical education to the artistic element as well. We will turn gymnastics and movement games into expressions of emotions that are stimulated by music or recitation. Meaningful eurythmic movement will replace movement that depends only on anatomical and physiological aspects of the body. We will find that a very strong force shapes the will and the feelings when we compose our classroom instruction artistically. However, only teachers whose keen understanding of the human being permits them to see the connection between their methods and the developmental forces that reveal themselves at a specific stage of life will be able to teach really fruitfully in the way described here. The true teachers and educators are not those who have learned pedagogy as the science of dealing with children, but those in whom pedagogy has awakened through understanding the human being.

For the emotional development of children under the age of nine, it is important that they develop their relationship to the world as people tend to do when they conceive of it imaginatively. If teachers themselves are not idle dreamers, they will not turn the children into dreamers simply by allowing the world of plants, animals, air, and stars to live in the hearts and minds of the children in the form of a fairy-tale or fable.

Visual instruction is certainly justified within certain limits. However, if our materialistic viewpoint makes us want to extend it to virtually everything, we fail to take into account the fact that the human being must also develop forces that cannot be imparted solely through the ability to visualize. For example, learning certain things purely through memory is related to the developmental forces that are present between the sixth or seventh year and the fourteenth year of life. This quality of human nature is what mathematical instruction should be based on. It can even be used to cultivate the power of memory. If we do not take this into account, we may emphasize the visual over the memory-strengthening element in our math lessons in an unpedagogical way.

It is possible to fall into the same mistake if we do not strike the right balance in our concern about having the children understand everything we convey to them at every opportunity. This concern is certainly underlain by good will, but it does not take into account what it means for people later on in life when something they learned purely by rote at an earlier stage reawakens in their souls, and they find that they now understand it out of themselves because of the maturity they have gained. We may be afraid that rote learning of subject matter will result in lack of participation on the part of the students, and of course a life-filled manner on the part of the teacher will be necessary to prevent this. If teachers are present in their teaching activity with their full being, then it is permissible for them to convey something to the children that will meet with full and joyful understanding only when it is re-experienced later. Inherent in this refreshing re-experience is a strengthening of the content of a person's life. If teachers can work to bring about a strengthening of this sort, they provide the children with immeasurably great wealth for their journey through life. They also avoid having their "visual instruction" fall into banality through over-attention to the children's "understanding"—a method whose fruits cannot be enjoyed beyond childhood even though the children's independent individual activity has been taken into account. Through things that are still beyond their understanding in some respect, an awakening force is enkindled in the children by the teacher's living ardor. This force will remain effective throughout their entire lives.

  * If after the end of the children's ninth year we begin describing nature, the animal and plant worlds, in a way that makes human forms and phenomena of human life understandable through forms and life processes in the world outside of the human being, this can awaken in our students the forces that are striving for emancipation from the depths of human nature at this stage of life. Corresponding to the character of

the children's feeling of ego identity at this stage of life, we see the animal and plant kingdoms as distributing among many species of beings the characteristics and routine actions that are revealed in the human being, the apex of the living world, as a harmonious unity.

Around the twelfth year of life, another turning point in human development sets in. A person of this age is ready to develop the capabilities that lead in an individually advantageous way to grasping things that must be understood totally without reference to the human being: the mineral kingdom, the phenomena of the world of physics, meteorological phenomena, and so forth.

Exercises in these subjects are developed on the basis of the nature of the human urge to be active, and without regard for the goals of practical life, yet from them other lessons develop that constitute a type of instruction in work. This results from understanding the character of the different stages of life. What has been indicated here with regard to individual areas of study can be extended to everything that is to be imparted to the students up to their fifteenth year of life.

If we pay attention in the way that has been described to the educational principles that result from the inner development of the human being, we need not fear that students will leave primary school with constitutions of body and soul that are foreign to outer life. Our life itself takes shape out of individuals' inner development, and the best possible way of entering it is for people to develop their potentials and link them to what their predecessors incorporated into civilization as it developed as a result of similar individual potentials. Of course, in order for the students' development and the outer development of civilization to coincide, we need a faculty whose interest is not limited to specialized educational practices. Rather, this faculty must be fully involved in the broader aspects of life. A faculty of this sort will find it possible to awaken in people who are growing up, not only a sense for life's spiritual and intellectual substance, but also an understanding of its practical organization. When taught in this way, fourteen or fifteen-year-olds will not lack understanding of the essential aspects of agriculture, industry and commerce that serve the overall life of humankind. The insights and capabilities that they have acquired will enable them to feel oriented in the life that embraces them.

If the Waldorf School is to achieve the goals that its founders have in mind, it will have to build upon the educational theory and methods that have been described here. They will enable it to provide an education that allows the bodies of the students to develop healthily and in accordance with their needs because the souls of which these bodies are expressions are unfolding in line with their developmental forces. The way we attempted to work with the faculty before the school opened will enable the school to strive toward a goal such as that given here.[3] Those who worked to establish the school believe that the goal that has been set leads into a pedagogical realm of life that corresponds to our contemporary way of thinking about society. They feel the responsibility that must be associated with an attempt of this sort, but are of the opinion that in the face of the social challenges presented by our times, it is their duty to undertake such a thing when the possibility presents itself.

---

3. Work with the teachers prior to the opening of the school: In the time between August 21 and September 5, 1919, Rudolf Steiner gave three lecture courses: *Allgemeine Menschenkunde* (GA 293), previously, *The Study of Man*, presently, *The Foundations of Human Experience*, Anthroposophic Press, Hudson, NY, 1996; *Erziehungskunst. Methodisch-Didaktisches* (GA 294) *Practical Advice to Teachers*, Rudolf Steiner Press, London, 1976; and *Erziehungskunst. Seminarbesprechungen und Lehrplanvorträge* (GA 295) *Discussions with Teachers*, Anthroposophic Press, Hudson, NY, 1996.

Speech by councilor of commerce Emil Molt at the opening of the Independent Waldorf School in the *Stadtgartensaal*, Stuttgart [4]

September 7, 1919

Ladies and gentlemen; dear children! In the name of my company, the Waldorf-Astoria, I extend a cordial welcome to all of you who have come here to take part in this simple little opening ceremony for our Waldorf School. I would especially like to heartily welcome our honored guests. I want to thank them for putting in an appearance here today and for the interest in our undertaking that this demonstrates.

Ladies and gentlemen! Founding the Waldorf School was not something that sprang from the mere quirk of an individual. Rather, the idea was born out of insight into the needs of our present time. I simply felt the need to truly call the first so-called "comprehensive school" into existence and thereby to alleviate a social need, so that in future not only the sons and daughters of the affluent but also the children of simple workers will be in a position to acquire the education that is needed nowadays to ascend to a higher level of culture. In this sense, it is a deep personal satisfaction to me that it has been possible to call this institution into existence. But today it is not enough to simply create a facility; it is also necessary to fill it with a new spirit. And anthroposophically oriented spiritual science is our guarantee that a spirit of this sort will fill this facility. I feel a

---

4. This address was published in the *Waldorf-Nachrichten* [Waldorf News], vol.1, no.19, October 1919.

deep inner responsibility at this point to express heartfelt thanks to the one who has conveyed this spiritual science to us, our beloved Dr. Rudolf Steiner. But I also thank the authorities who have made it possible for us to bring this facility into existence, so that we are in the fortunate position today of really turning our thoughts into deeds.

But now I turn especially to you, dear staff and managers of the Waldorf-Astoria Company: Let us be clear that by calling such a thing into existence, we also take on a great responsibility. Let us be clear on this, and let us solemnly swear and promise today to show ourselves worthy to be the first in the German Empire to have the possibility of enacting this idea of the comprehensive school, which has been spoken about so much, right here in our city of Stuttgart. Let us show the world that we are not only idealists, but also people of practical deeds, and that our children, strengthened by this school, will in future be able to cope with daily life in a better and fuller manner.

It is in this sense that we send you, dear children, to this Waldorf School, so that when you leave this place you may draw from it the strength to cope, as whole human beings, with the difficult life that awaits you. But there are also joys that await you in this school. I was privileged to take part in the course that Dr. Steiner gave for the teachers, and so I became very aware of how much we ourselves missed out on in our youth, and how difficult it is later on in life to make up for what we missed back then. It is truly a matter dear to my heart to say that since we ourselves were not in a position to enjoy this blessing in earlier times, we must at least thank our destiny that we can make it available for others today. And thus I can say to you children who are entering this new school that there are pleasures waiting for you. And those who were privileged to take the course that Dr.Steiner gave for the new teachers know that this new method means that learning will no longer be a pain for you as it was for us older ones; for you, it will be a joy and a pleasure. So be glad, children, that you will be allowed to enjoy this school. You may not be able to understand this today in all its implications, but when you graduate from this place of education, show that you are a match for life and its challenges, show the world the wonderful fruits of this new method of education that will teach you to be purposeful individuals able to cope with life.

We also realize, however, that what we can create here is just a small beginning. The responsibility is great and the burden rests heavily on those who have accepted this task, and as time passes the attacks that come from all sides may also be great, but there is one thing we can already say today: The will within us will be so strong and the thoughts so mighty and the courage so great that we will also be able to overcome all the things that may try to hinder us, because we know what a lofty goal we are striving for, and because we are always aware of the responsibility that we have taken on.

And you, dear teachers who have taken up this work, who have yourselves been introduced to the spirit that is to ensoul this school, you know what a great responsibility has been laid upon you, and I address this request to all of you who will participate as faculty in the Waldorf School—may you all, along with me, be aware of the extraordinary gravity of this responsibility, and may you never cease to feel this responsibility as deeply as I do at all times.

And now, ladies and gentlemen, in handing over this institute to the staff and management of the Waldorf-Astoria company, and thus also to the public, I wish from the bottom of my heart that the spirit that brought us a Goethe, a Schiller, a Herder and whatever their names may be, all those great cultural heroes of the past, that this spirit may reign here again, so that through the school of the future this spirit can once again enter our German fatherland. If this is the case, then all of us who carry the responsibility for it will be aware that we are the servants of these spiritual forces. Then a day will dawn when our poor fatherland can begin to ascend from the depths of its great need, both of body and of soul, and we may hope that then there will be more people who can help to lead our people upward to the heights where our cultural heroes, a Goethe and a Schiller and so forth, once stood, and further still.

And in once again expressing my wish that this undertaking of ours may happily thrive, I do solemnly swear and promise in the name of the Waldorf staff, in the name of our school, in the name of our children, that this school will become a garden and a fountain of everything that is good, beautiful and true.

Speech by Rudolf Steiner at the opening of the Independent Waldorf School

September 7, 1919

Ladies and gentlemen! From Herr Molt's words, you will have inferred out of what spirit he took the initiative to found this Waldorf School. You will also have gathered from his words that its founding springs, not from any mundane intention, but from a call that resounds very clearly from the evolution of humanity in our times in particular. And yet, so little of this call is heard. Humanity's evolution resounds with much that can be encompassed within the framework of rebuilding society, of giving social form to humanity's lot. Thus there is something in this call, above all else, that must not be disregarded: the issue of education. We can rest assured that the only people who hear this call for social restructuring correctly amid the chaos of what our present time demands of us will be those who pursue its consequences all the way to the issue of education. But we will certainly be on the wrong track if we hear this social call in a way that makes us want to call a halt to all our social striving when faced with the issue of education, preferring to fashion the facilities of our educational system on the basis of social principles, whatever they may be, that have not also sprung from a renewal of the source of education.

For me, ladies and gentlemen, it has been a sacred obligation to take up what lay in our friend Herr Molt's intentions in founding the Waldorf School, and to do so in a way that enabled this school to be fashioned out of what we believe to have won from spiritual science in our present times. This school is really intended to be integrated into what the evolution of humanity requires of us at present and in the near future. Actually, in the end, everything that flows into the educational system from such requirements constitutes a threefold sacred obligation.

Of what use would be all of the human community's feeling, understanding, and working if these could not condense into the sacred responsibility taken on by teachers in their specific social communities when they embark on the ultimate community service with children, with people who are growing up and in the becoming? In the end, everything we are capable of knowing about human beings and about the world only really becomes fruitful when we can convey it in a living way to those who will fashion society when we ourselves can no longer contribute our physical work.

Everything we can accomplish artistically only achieves its highest good when we let it flow into the greatest of all art forms, the art in which we are given, not a dead medium such as sound or color, but living human beings, incomplete and imperfect, whom we are to transform to some extent, through art and education, into accomplished human beings.

And is it not ultimately a very holy and religious obligation to cultivate and educate the divine spiritual element that manifests anew in every human being who is born? Is this educational service not a religious service in the highest sense of the word? Is it not so that all the holiest stirrings of humanity, which we dedicate to religious feeling, must come together in our service at the altar when we attempt to cultivate the divine spiritual aspect of the human being whose potentials are revealed in the growing child?

Science that comes alive!

Art that comes alive!

Religion that comes alive!

In the end, that is what education is.

If we understand teaching and child-rearing in this sense, we will not be inclined to carelessly criticize what is imposed from the other side as the principles, goals, and foundations of the art of education. However, it does seem to me that no proper insight into what our modern culture demands of the art of education is possible unless we are aware of the great need for a complete spiritual renewal in our times, unless we can really work our way through to understanding that in future, something must flow into what we do as teachers and educators that is quite different from what can thrive in the sphere of what is now known as "scientific education." Nowadays, after all, future teachers, people who will have a formative influence on human beings, are introduced to the attitudes and way of thinking of contemporary science. Now, it has never occurred to me to denigrate contemporary science. I am full of regard for all the triumphs it has achieved, and will continue to achieve for the sake of humanity's evolution, through a scientific viewpoint and method that are based on understanding nature. But for that very reason, it seems to me, what comes from the contemporary scientific and intellectual attitude cannot be fruitfully applied to the art of education. Its greatness does not lie in dealing with human beings or in insight into the human heart and mind. Great technical advances are possible as a result of what springs from our contemporary intellectual attitude, and on that same basis it is also possible to develop the basic convictions of a free humanity in the context of society. However, it is not possible—grotesque as this may still sound to the majority of people today—to take a scientific viewpoint that has gradually come to the conclusion that the human heart is a pump and the human body a mechanical device, to use the feelings and sensations that proceed from this science to inspire us to become artistic educators of growing human beings. It is impossible to develop the living art of education out of what makes our times so great in mastering dead technology.

This, ladies and gentlemen, is where a new spirit must enter the evolution of humanity—the spirit we seek through our spiritual science, the spirit that leads us away from seeing the living human being as a carrier of implements that pump and suck, as a mechanism that can only be understood according to the methods of natural science. Into this intellectual attitude of humanity must come the conviction that spirit is alive in all natural existence, and that we are capable of recognizing this spirit. This is why, in the course that preceded this Waldorf venture, in the course intended for teachers, we attempted to found an anthropology or science of education that will develop into an art of education and a study of humanity that will once again raise what is alive in the human being from the dead. The dead—and this is the secret of our dying contemporary culture—is what makes people knowing, what gives them insight when they take it up as natural law. However, it also weakens the feeling that is the source of teachers' inspiration and enthusiasm, and it weakens the will. It does not grant human beings a harmonious place within society as a whole. We are looking for a science that is not mere science, that is itself life and feeling. When such a science streams into the human soul as knowledge, it will immediately develop the power to be active as love and to stream forth as effective, working will, as work that has been steeped in soul warmth, and especially as work that applies to the living, to the growing human being. We need a new scientific attitude. Above all, we need a new spirit for the entire art of education.

Ladies and gentlemen, if we think about contemporary education and its needs, we will not be too quick to criticize what has been undertaken with the best of intentions on the basis of all kinds of worthwhile impulses, both in the present and in the recent past. What beautiful impulses underlay the efforts to move the educational system out of the chaos and deadening aspects of city life to the country, to rural boarding schools! We must acknowledge all the good will that was expended in this direction. However, ladies and gentlemen, if the living spirit that makes the human being comprehensible to human beings, that shows people how to deal with the growing human being, does not enter these rural boarding schools, then what was dead in the cities remains dead in the country.

People are now considering how to draft a constitution for a school so that the teachers' authority would no longer work in a deadening way. However, if they are unable to inject the real living spirit that makes human beings human into these newly structured schools, then in spite of all their socio-educational theories these educational establishments will remain something dead, something that cannot lead the present generation into the future in the right way.

The conviction that the call resounding from humanity's evolution demands a new spirit for our present age, and that we must carry this spirit into the school system first and fore-most, is what underlies the efforts of this Waldorf School, which is intended to be a model along these lines. An effort has been made to listen to what is subconsciously present in the demands of the best of those who have attempted to work for healing and regeneration of the art of education in the recent past. In this context I had to think of explanations given by Theodor Vogt, a student of Herbart's and a prolific thinker, and by his successor Rein, professor of education at Jena.[5] Their thoughts seem to me to spring from a deeper feeling for what is lacking in our educational system at present. Vogt and Rein suspected, although they did not clearly say it, that in order to really be able to educate, it would be desirable to know how children actually develop in the early years between infancy and the time they enter school around the seventh year of life, and above all how they develop during the primary school years, from their sixth or seventh year of life up to the time in their fourteenth or fifteenth year that impacts so heavily on the growing person's entire development. Insightful instructors of education ask whether we can also understand the kinds of forces at work in human nature, which presents us with a different intellectual, emotional, and bodily face, if not every month, then at least every year. As long as we have no real science of history, so these educators say, we will also not be able to know how an individual human being develops, because the individual human being presents in concentrated form what humanity as a whole has gone through in the course of its historical development.

People like the ones I mentioned felt that modern science is basically a failure when it comes to saying anything about the

---

5. Theodor Vogt, 1835-1906. Wilhelm Rein, 1847-1929, author of *Päda-gogik im Grundriss* [An Outline of Pedagogy].

great laws that prevail throughout history, or to grasping what wells up out of the great all-encompassing laws of human evolution for us at the present moment. We would be attempting to do something very foolish if we tried to understand individual human beings on the basis of the composition of the nutrients they take in from their first breath until their last. However, this is basically what we are trying to do in the case of history, in understanding humanity's entire evolution. In the case of an individual, we must understand how a physiological process such as the change of teeth intervenes in development, for example. We must know all the mysterious things that are going on in the body as a result of a completely new physiology that is not yet available to modern science. But we must also know what is accompanying this transformation on an emotional level. We must know about the metamorphoses of human nature. In the case of an individual, we will at least not deny, although we may be powerless to fully recognize the fact, that a person experiences metamorphoses or transformations on the basis of his or her inmost being. We do not admit to this with regard to the historical development of humanity as a whole. The same methods are applied to antiquity, the Middle Ages, and recent times. We do not accept that great leaps have taken place in humanity's historical evolution. Looking back over historical developments, we find the last leap in the fifteenth century. Humanity's ways of feeling, conceptualizing, and willing, as they have developed in more recent times and as we know them now, have only taken on this subtle character among civilized humanity since the fifteenth century. How this civilized humanity differs from that of the tenth or eighth century is similar to how a twelve-year-old child differs from a child who has not yet reached his or her seventh year. And what happened by way of transformation in the fifteenth century proceeded from the innermost nature of humanity, just as the change of teeth as a lawful development proceeds from the innermost nature of the individual. And everything we are living with now in the twentieth century—our striving for individuality, the striving for new social forms, the striving to develop the personality—is only a consequence of what the inner forces of history have brought up since the time in question.

We can understand how individuals attempt to take their place in the present only if we understand the course that humanity's development has taken, as described above. People like Vogt and Rein who have given a lot of thought to education and who have also been involved practically in such things know that the powerlessness of our modern art of education is a result of the powerlessness of modern historical insight. Just as it is impossible to educate human beings with a science for which the heart has become a pump, it is also impossible to find one's place as a teacher in a system of education based on a historical understanding that does not draw on the living spirit of humanity or recognize the metamorphoses that have taken place between the Middle Ages and modern times. We are still involved with the consequences of what began there.

Regardless of the fact that we tend to make fun of prophecy in this day and age, it must be said that in a certain respect teachers must be prophets. After all, they are dealing with what is meant to live in the generation to come, not in the present.

From the insightful vantage point of real, true historical happenings, ladies and gentlemen, such things often look somewhat different than they do to modern observers of humanity. In many respects, these observers often have a very superficial grasp of what is meant to come to life in the science and art of education. Today the question is being debated of whether people should be educated more in line with what fosters human nature itself—that is, whether a more humanistic education is preferable—or whether they should be provided with an education that prepares them for their future careers and to fit into the context of the state, and so on. For those who attempt an insight into the depths of such things, discussions of this sort are verbal dialectics that take place on the surface. Why is that? Those with insight into the generation to come get a clear feeling that individuals, in what they work at, think, and feel, and in what they strive toward for the future as adults, emanate from the womb of history. Careers and state context and the places people can make for themselves—all this originated in these people themselves. It is not something external that is superimposed on them. We cannot ask whether we should have the individual being or the outer career more in view when we educate people, because if seen rightly, these are one and the same thing!

If we can develop a living understanding of the careers and people that are out there, then we can also develop an understanding of what previous generations that are still alive and at work today brought up out of the womb of humanity into the present time.

Separating education toward a career and education toward being an individual is not sufficient when we want to work as teachers and educators. There needs to be something living in us that is not outwardly visible, neither in a career nor in the context of the state nor anywhere else in the outer world. What must be alive in us is what the generations to come will bring to life's outer level. What must live in us is a prophetic merging with the future evolution of humanity. The educational and artistic feeling, thinking and willing of a faculty stands and falls with this merging. A living theory and methodology of education for the present must strive to have flow into the faculty what can be known about the growing human being. This is like a soul and spiritual life-blood that becomes art without first having been knowledge. What is to enter the childlike heart, mind, and intellect can proceed only from this living methodology.

I cannot present our educational principles in detail today. I only wanted to point out how the art of education as it is meant to be in the present and future is to take its place in a living spiritual grasp of the entire nature of the world and of humanity.

We talk a lot today about the social forms of humanity's future. Why is it always so difficult to take steps to bring this future about? It is difficult because in our times, antisocial drives and instincts are present in the evolution of humanity and work against social striving.

When we look back at patriarchal times, to a time when humanity led a more instinctive life than is the case in our civilization, we may have many reasons to be proud of the accomplishments of the present. However, the impulses of earlier times were more social than ours; we are now governed by antisocial impulses. These antisocial impulses, however, must be eliminated from the art of education above all else. More precise observers will note how our educational system has gradually developed into an antisocial system. However, the only art of education that can be fruitful is one in which the teacher's effect on the child results from a commonality of feeling from the very moment they enter the classroom. The child's soul and the teacher's soul must become one through a mysterious and subconscious bond that passes from the teacher's spirit to the child's. This gives the school its social character. For this to happen, the teacher must be able to put him or herself in the child's position.

What do we often do nowadays? We make an effort to formulate our thoughts in ways that will enable us to explain something to the children. Perhaps we say to them, "Look, here is a chrysalis. A butterfly is going to come out of it." We may show the children the butterfly and the chrysalis and may also demonstrate how the one develops out of the other. Perhaps we then go on to say, "Your immortal souls are at rest in your bodies just as the butterfly is at rest in the chrysalis. And just as the butterfly leaves the chrysalis one day, so too your immortal souls will one day leave your bodies when you go through the gate of death." We have thought of an image from nature that we use in order to make something clear to the children, but we know that we have only used a comparison, and that we ourselves have a different way of understanding the whole thing. We have made an effort to straighten something out for the children. However, according to a mysterious law, we cannot really accomplish anything in the lesson if we straighten things out in this way. It is really only possible to convey to the children what we ourselves believe in the depths of our souls. Only when we have wrestled our way through to the feeling that the image of the butterfly and chrysalis is no mere cooked-up comparison, but one presented to us by divine spiritual nature itself, only when we can believe in the truth of the image in the way that the children are meant to believe it, only in that instant are we able to convey living spirit to them.

It is never permissible for us to merely give lip service to something, although this plays such a great role in cultural development today. We must speak and be able to work out of the spirit of truth. This is possible only when we are connected, deeply and intimately connected, to everything human. Even if we are already white-haired, we must be able to unite with what growing human beings are in accordance with their essential nature. We must have an inner understanding of the growing human being. Can we still do that today? No, we cannot, or we would not sit ourselves down in laboratories and practice experimental psychology in order to work out the rules by which human understanding and human memory work. If teachers see these superficial methods and procedures as the essential thing in learning to understand the human being, they kill off their living intuitive connection and relationship to human beings. I know that educational experiments and experimental psychology are useful to teachers in a certain way. However, I also know that these are only symptoms of what they are supposed to be most useful for, and I know that we have lost the direct soul-route from person to person and are looking for it again through outer observation in laboratories. We have become inwardly estranged from what is human and are looking for it in outer ways. However, if we want to be real teachers and educators, we must be reunited with the human aspect. We must foster the whole person within us, and then this whole person will be related to what we have to develop in the child in educational and artistic ways. What we as educators gain from experimental study and observation, which are often promoted as the basis of the science of education nowadays, is comparable to the effort of trying to understand how we eat and drink on the basis of the study of nutrition and its applications to the human being. We do not need a science of how one eats and drinks, we need a healthily developed sense of taste and healthy organs, and then we will eat and drink properly. Nor do we need a theory of education based on experimental psychology. What we as educators need is an awakening of our living human nature, which will experience in itself the whole of the child to which it makes a spiritual connection.

And so, ladies and gentlemen, we want to create this Waldorf School on the basis of a new spirit. You will also have noticed what this school is *not* meant to become. In any case, it is not meant to become a school to promote a particular philosophy. Anyone who says that anthroposophically oriented spiritual science is founding the Waldorf School, and that it is now going to inject its philosophy into this school, will not be speaking the truth. I am stating this now, on the opening day. We are not interested in imposing our "dogmas," our principles, or the content of our world-view on young people. We are not trying to bring about a dogmatic form of education. We are striving to turn what we have been able to learn from spiritual science into a living act of education. We are striving to include in our instructional methods a way of dealing with individual souls that can originate in a living spiritual science. Dead science can give rise only to knowledge; living spiritual science will give rise to instructional methodology and practical applications in the soul-spiritual sense. We strive to teach, to be able to educate. With regard to all this, we are fundamentally aware of the responsibility our dear friend Herr Molt spoke of earlier. We have pledged that the various religious denominations will be able to provide religious instruction in the school and to introduce the principles of their world-views, and we will honor this promise. It remains to be seen whether the art form we want to introduce provisorily and in a modest way will encounter as little interference from them as the world-views which they introduce will encounter from us.[6] We know that before humankind can acquire a correct insight into issues involving world-views and their interrelationships, people must understand that an art of education in the pedagogical and methodological sense can result from a spiritual world-view. Thus, we are not going to found a school on the basis of a particular world-view. What we are attempting to create in the Waldorf School is a school based on the art of education.

---

6. Unlike in the U.S., in Germany it is even now quite standard for state-supported schools to make space available in the school and time in the school week for religious instruction, with teachers supplied by the churches.

To you parents of the first children to be sent to this school, let me say that you are pioneering not only a personal human intention, but also a cultural challenge of our times, and that you will be able to grasp in the right way what is now meant to happen with regard to the Waldorf School only if you feel yourselves to be pioneers of this sort.

It is too soon to speak to the children in words as rational as those I spoke to their parents, but we will promise these children that what we are conveying to their parents in words will come to them in the form of actions—actions that will help them find their place in life so that they will be a match for the difficult challenges facing the generations to come. These challenges will be difficult, and what we today, especially in Central Europe, are experiencing as a time of great troubles is only the beginning of greater troubles to come. But just as the greatest things for human beings have always emerged from pain and suffering, so too a true, reality-based human art of education will emerge from these troubles. By seeking the source and foundation of our school system in the whole human being, by trying to build it up on the basis of the whole human being, we want to insert the social issue of education into the overall social issue of our times.

Comprehensive school! That is what our times are saying. And the art of teaching that draws its ability from the whole human being, as has been indicated here, will appear only in a comprehensive school. If humanity is to be able to live in social justice in the future, then people must first educate their children in a socially appropriate way. Through the Waldorf School, we hope to make a small contribution toward bringing this about.

In spite of the best will, we may be able to accomplish only a portion of what we set out to do, but we hope that the strength of the effort may not be exhausted in our feeble attempts, and that it will find successors. For we are convinced that although a feeble attempt may fail due to opposition and lack of under-standing, the central core of this effort will find successors. When a real social art of education finds its way into the con-sciousness of all of humanity, which is what carries the faculty and the group of children to be educated, then the school will be incorporated into our overall life in society in the right way.

May the Waldorf School make a small contribution toward this great goal.

Address at the Christmas Assembly

December 21, 1919

Dear children! Several weeks ago, when we all came to this school for the first time, I visited you more often. Then there were a few weeks when I had to be quite far away from here, but each morning when I got up and went to work, I won-dered, "What are my dear Waldorf children and their teachers doing now?" This thought came to me often during the day. And now, in the festive Christmas season, I have had the privi-lege of being able to visit you again. I went into all your classes and asked many of you, "Do you love your teachers?" ["Yes!" shout the children.] And you see, you answered me warmly, just like that. And then I said to you, "That is an especially nice Christmas gift for me!"

And it is a nice Christmas gift for me. You see, dear children, I have to think about how you have been spending your days since Herr Molt gave us the gift of this Waldorf School. After resting from evening until morning in the divine spirit that watches over your souls from the time you go to sleep until the time you wake up, and after you have washed and dressed and gotten all ready, you come up here to this beautiful schoolhouse. And I believe that many of you, maybe even all of you, look forward to everything that will be here for you in this beautiful schoolhouse. ["Yes!" shout the children.]

Dear children, you have reason to look forward to it. You see, while I was away from you I thought of you often, and in my thoughts I wondered, "What are my dear Waldorf children doing?" And I also said to myself, "They will be doing just fine, because they have nice capable teachers, and these nice capable teachers approach them with real love and are working very hard so that something good will come of the children." And then I had to think of how you look forward to coming up here and of the love you show for your teachers. These teachers have to work long and hard to be able to teach you all the good and beautiful things that will make good and capable people out of you.

And you know, my dear children, I was especially pleased when I was in the classes and some children would come in playing the part of Ruprecht[7] or of little angels, and they sang and talked about the child Jesus, about the holy Christ Child. It was beautiful and grand that you could speak about the Christ with such love, and that you could listen with such love.

And do you know where your teachers get all the strength and ability they need so that they can teach you to grow up to be good and capable people? They get it from the Christ, whom we think about at Christmas. We think about how He came into the world to bring joy to all people, and you gave some beautiful presentations about Him today.

---

7. Ruprecht: in the European tradition, the Moorish helper of St. Nicholas, who carries a black sack and administers symbolic punishments to children who have been bad during the past year.

You see, my dear children, there are beings on earth that are not like human beings—for example, the animals around us—and we might often think that we should envy these animals. You can look up and see the birds flying, and perhaps then you might say, "Oh, if only we could fly, too! Then we would be able to soar into the air." We human beings cannot fly like the birds because we have no wings. However, dear children, we can fly into the element of the spiritual, and we have two wings to fly there. The wing on the left is called "hard work," and the other wing on the right is called "paying attention." We cannot see them, but these two wings—hard work and paying attention—make it possible for us to fly into life and become people who are really ready for life. If we work hard and pay attention as children, and if we have teachers that are as good and capable as yours, then what makes us fit for life will come to us, and on the wings of hard work and paying attention we will be able to fly into life, where the love of our teachers carries us.

You know, you can sometimes think that there are things that are more fun than learning. But that is not really true; there is no greater joy than learning. You see, when you enjoy something that lets you be inattentive and does not make you work hard, then the joy is over immediately. You enjoy it, and then the joy is gone. But when you enjoy what you can learn, when you are flying on the wings of hard work and paying attention, then, my dear children, something stays behind in your souls. (Later on you will know what the soul is.) Something stays in your soul, and you can enjoy that over and over again. When we have learned something good and proper, it comes back again and again; we enjoy it again and again with a joy that never stops. But the other fun things, the ones that come only from inattentiveness and laziness, they come to an end.

You see, because many of you—all of you, I would like to believe—want to work hard and pay attention to what your nice teachers are giving you, I was so glad to see your love for your teachers streaming out of your eyes when I saw you again. And so that you do not forget it, I would like to ask you again, "Don't you all sincerely love your teachers?" ["Yes, we do!" shout the children.] Now, that is what you should always say. That is what you should always feel, and then the spirit whose earthly life and birth we remember at Christmas time, the Christ spirit, will take joy in you.

Now, my dear children, when you have felt your teachers' love all day long up here, then you can go home again and tell your parents about what you have learned, and your parents will be glad and say to themselves, "Well, our children are going to grow up to be good and capable people."

Make sure to write that in your souls, for now is a good time to do that. When we think of the great festival that reminds us that the Christ entered our world to bring comfort and joy to all human beings who turn their hearts and souls toward Him, then we can also inscribe in our souls the intention to become good human beings. Because the power of Christ is helping you, you will become what you write in your souls today, what you seriously intend to become. And when I come again and see that you have made even more progress, when I come again and see that you can once again show me that you have taken love for your teachers into your hearts and kept it there, then I will again be very glad. My warmest Christmas wish for you today is that this love will grow ever more perfect in you, and that you may continue to unfold the left wing of the human soul, which is hard work, and the right wing, which is paying attention.

And now that I have spoken to the children, let me still say a few words to those who have accompanied them here. What I just said to the children flows from a deeply satisfied heart, because I really have received the most beautiful Christmas greeting from them. When I came into the school, what wafted toward me was something I would like to call the good spirit of this school. It was the really good spirit, the good and unifying spirit, that brings teachers and children together here.

You see, in these days a Christmas mood was resting on all the serious teaching that was taking place, and it was deeply satisfying to perceive this Christmas mood, into which the revelation of Christ speaks, if I may put it like that, in all the corridors and especially in the classrooms. This was no mere supplement to the regular lessons. You could feel that our faculty managed to warm and enlighten everything that was being presented to the children's souls and hearts and understanding with the real, true spirit of Christ. Here, in accordance with the wishes of the divine spirit, we do not speak the name of Christ after every sentence—for "Thou shalt not take the name of the Lord thy God in vain!"—but it is nonetheless true that this spirit of Christ is with us in all our individual subjects and in every teaching activity. This is something that can readily be felt, especially at this time of year. Perhaps you too have been able to feel it in what came to meet you out of this Christmas assembly.

And finally, to conclude my Christmas greeting, I would like to appeal to the children whom you have sent here. I hope their progress pleases you.

Children, when you enter these rooms with the other boys and girls, recall that you are meant to love each other warmly, to love each and every other one. If love prevails among you, you will thrive under the care of your teachers, and your parents at home will have no concerns and will have loving thoughts of how you are spending your time here.

There is something we may say today, ladies and gentlemen, which should resound, as the spirit of this school, from every word and glance the children bring home to you who have sent them here, as an echo of what is meant to permeate all of our human journeying on earth since the mystery of Golgotha took place, to permeate all human work and activity, and especially all activity in which the spirit has work to do. May the words that ring in our souls today weave through everything that human beings do out of self-understanding, weave like a warming breath of air or beam of sunlight:

The revelation of the divine from heavenly heights,
And peace to human beings on earth who are of good will![8]

Our great ideal is to cultivate this good will in the children of the Waldorf School. Our concern must be to find the governance of the spirit of the world in our work, in everything we do. May the Christmas message, "The revelation of the spirit of God from the heavenly heights, and peace to human beings on earth who are of good will," trickle down into all the work of the Waldorf School as well. May the school's working strength be governed by brotherly love and by the peace that inspires and supports all work! That, dear ladies and gentlemen, is my Christmas greeting to you today.

---

8. A free rendering of the angels' words to the shepherds (Luke 2:14).

1 9 2 0

Address at a monthly assembly[1]

June 10, 1920

Dear children! Last time I was able to be here, I told you how glad I am when our dear friend Herr Molt comes to pick me up in Dornach, where the school for big people, for grown-ups, is being built.[2] Then I can be with you again for a little while and see what you are doing.

And why am I so glad when Herr Molt comes to bring me here? Because it makes me think, "Now I am going to the school that was founded for our dear children"—that is, for you who are here because you long to become capable people who are ready for life.

Because I have only been here for a short time, I have not been able to see much yet—just the tiny little folks in the first grade, and the eighth grade—but what I did see gave me great pleasure. I saw how patiently and lovingly the first grade teacher had helped the children make some progress, and I was privileged to spend a very nice lesson with the eighth grade

---

1. Rudolf Steiner had suggested that the students gather at the school for a brief celebration instead of the monthly day off from school that was the custom in Baden-Württemberg. The mood of the course of the year was to form the background for this event and the classes were to show each other what they had been working on in recitation, drama, music, and eurythmy, or in foreign languages, gymnastics, and so on. Rudolf Steiner also gave a talk at these assemblies whenever he could be in Stuttgart.
2. The wooden building of the Goetheanum, the Free School of Spiritual Science, was under construction from 1913–1921.

students. They were hearing about what human history tells us of how human beings on earth are involved in an evolution, an ongoing progress, that is driven by the spirit: Something that lives in human history gives us the desire to work on into the future. The spirit in which this was being conveyed to the souls of our dear young friends in the eighth grade was very beautiful. I am looking forward to seeing all the other classes, too. I am always pleased when I see how what our friend Herr Molt planted here is beginning to develop.

You entered this school when the fall was approaching. At that time we tried to think about what we would experience here and what we wanted to foster—love for each other, love for our teachers, love for God, who speaks to us from everything. And now, while you have been enjoying what your teachers presented to you each morning, you have also been experiencing what comes up out of the earth, what the spring draws out of it. You have seen the trees growing green. And now we remember what we hear when we go out into the woods. We hear the songbirds, and we are glad.

But today we have also heard something else, something for which I am especially thankful. We have heard you, under the direction of your teachers, express something that comes from inside of you. We can hear the birds singing out in the woods, and we can also hear what you have expressed to us, but there is a difference between them.

We are glad when we hear the little birds singing. But we know that something else is present when we hear what you perform for us. This is something that we call the human soul. It is your human souls that speak to us and sing to us. This is what human beings make out of what speaks to them out there in nature. In the woods, we hear the birds, but when you sing many other things that are heard come toward us out from the human soul.

But there are also other things out there in nature. You see how the plants grow and the trees turn green. All of this is called forth by the light. Light floods the entire universe. Light and warmth are what call everything up out of the earth, all those things that delight your eyes and hearts. What sounds in your ears, brought to you through the patience and persistence of your teachers, what travels through the world as light and then enters your eyes—we hear all of this resounding from you, not only when you sing and dance, but also when you tell what you have learned to calculate and what you have learned about everything that is human. In your souls, this turns to light. And just think what the plants would be without the sun. They would not be able to come out of the ground. They would always remain roots that would not be able to develop flowers, and it would be dark. This is what it would be like for you if you went through the world without ever finding a school where you could learn something. You would be like a plant that never finds the sun. The soul finds its sun in people from whom it can learn something.

This is why we are so glad that a school like this has been founded as a result of Herr Molt's insight, and why you are so glad to be able to be in a school that you love. Seek the light of the soul, just as the plants seek the light and warmth of the sun!

I do not want to always say the same things to you, because I also do not want to always hear the same things when I come, but there is one thing that I want to hear from you again and again. You must answer me; this is what I am most curious about. And so I ask you, children, do you still love your teachers? ["Yes!" shout the children.] That is what I want to hear from the majority of you. That is what you are meant to take up into your souls. Love for your teachers will support you as you go out into life. Again and again, each time I come here, I would like to experience that you have made progress in learning, but I would also like you to show me that you have continued to love your teachers. You can be sure that in the great building that is being built for grown-ups in Dornach, where big people are meant to learn something, we all think about the Waldorf School here, and we think of it with love and joy. There are a lot of people who are thinking of the Waldorf School with love today, and they are thinking, "How good and capable these people will grow up to be, since as children they were filled with love for their teachers."

Oh, there is something I must tell you—Frau Steiner sends her greetings, since she cannot be here today.

There is a spirit that is always meant to prevail here, a spirit that your teachers bring to this place. From the spirit of the cosmos, they learn to bring this spirit here to you; they take in what St. Paul said with all of their souls. The spirit of Christ prevails throughout our school; whether we are doing arithmetic, reading, writing, or whatever we do, we do it with the attitude that the Christ awakened in us:

"I am with you always, even unto the end of the world."[3]

This is the spirit that is meant to prevail here, and it will do so through what your teachers bring to you with love, patience and endurance. May it also prevail through what lives in your souls!

Be with this spirit when you are in your class, and think of it when you leave. Be glad in your souls that you are coming back to the Waldorf School where the sun is lit for you, the sun that people need for life.

If there is someone among you who does not pay attention, there should be one of you who can go to that person and lovingly say, "Hey, hard work and paying attention get us up the mountain of life. Upward, friend! You should always be going

---

3. Matthew 28:20.

up the mountain of life."[4] This is how each of you should help the friend who falters a little—all of you for each one, all for one, one for all, lovingly. Love needs to be present among you, for each other and for your teachers. This is something we want to cultivate as part of the good spirit of the Waldorf School.

- -

Lecture given at a parents' evening:
Educational Practices in an Age of Decline and the Educational Practices of the Day to Come

June 11, 1920

Ladies and gentlemen! I would like to warmly welcome you here to this room, where we are gathered for the second time to relate important issues in the life of our Waldorf School. We are especially glad that so many of you have come. The theme I have chosen for tonight's lecture is "Educational Practices in an Age of Decline, and the Educational Practices of the Day to Come."

This is no mere theoretical problem for you, now that our Waldorf School has come into being. All the more reason for choosing a theme such as this, so it seemed to me. My remarks today are intended as an introductory formulation of this theme, which for you is not merely an intellectual problem but

---

4. In the original German, this is a reference to a song sung by the students at the beginning of the assembly.

an issue in which you discover real possibilities of entering into debate with our present times. Having decided, in the course of this debate, to send your children to the Waldorf school, you demonstrated your confidence in the new things this school is trying out. Taking your confidence as a basis, I would like to try to come to a conclusion of sorts by undertaking to illuminate everything that is falling away and dying off and now lies behind us, and by attempting to keep in mind the encouraging things that are coming towards us out of the work of the school up to this point.

In looking at this issue, it will be useful to keep in mind what the moment in which a child first enters school signifies under present circumstances. Circumstances being what they are today, we might say that the freshness and immediacy that are available to growing children at home have escaped from the compartmentalization and limitations that characterize our public life. The possibility for free human expression does exist at home, in the nursery. Not many contemporary children still have the possibility to give their energies free play in a way that corresponds to the deep urges of the individual nature of their will. That they will never again be able to do this is something that has developed over the last two centuries.

When children are sent out of this home environment to go to school, something happens that is very significant, of serious consequence in this day and age. No matter how much of the above-mentioned compartmentalized life we have been able to keep out of the nursery, it all lies in wait for the young person who is growing up. It begins to take effect on the very first day of school; it becomes relevant in the very moment the child enters school. Its effect is so great that it is no exaggeration to speak of a significant crisis in the life of the child.

This crisis consists of the child being confronted with a ready-made system of old educational practices that are in possession of something that is presented to the children in the form of a curriculum that is already worked out. This is fixed in the form of a comprehensive method that has been passed down to us, and in connection with its educational goals there is also a very specific way of enforcing discipline in school.

All of this is unfortunately structured in such a way that we cannot say that the actual driving forces of the present, especially the deeper currents of social change in the immediate past and in the present, have flowed into these structures at all. With regard to the curriculum, until just a few years ago it was generally the case that it existed in the form in which it had been drawn up fifty years ago. This contributed to lessening some negative consequences that could have proceeded from the curriculum. This will be touched on later.

Something was present in finished form, and we cannot say that the experience of people active in education had been able to flow into making it, since the people whose office entitled them to establish it may perhaps [only] have had a specific connection to the schools in the early stages of their development. Very soon this connection was severed, perhaps not by virtue of their outstanding quality as teachers, but because they had proven very adept at finding places in the school system's administration as up-and-coming officials who awakened hope. The so-called drawing-up of the curriculum as administered by these bureaucrats was cut off from the actual development of the schools themselves, although in fact we can hardly call it that. We might better speak of developmental forces being held back, as an attentive observer would have had to see.

From day one, the child was confronted with this curriculum, with something foreign and cold that determined with unrelenting strictness everything comprising the child's life of soul and spirit from the first day on. Not only the entire goal of teaching was already set, but in the last few decades it had even been determined at what stage instruction was supposed to be and at what date, from class to class and from week to week.

And how to reach this goal had been prescribed in detail through what was known as the state-approved method. This method was such that it was not possible for the individual teacher to freely disregard it. This would have been only briefly possible before he or she came into conflict with the officials who had to administrate this.

Now, how did this method work its way in? This method stems from presuppositions about human life that have basically been outdated for a long time. In the Middle Ages, schools developed under the sovereignty of the church. Then the states took over the ecclesiastical school system in its entirety and the state schools consolidated their position. The more their basis was prescribed in detail, the less possibility for evolution remained, we might say; the more the modern primary school was flaunted outwardly, the greater the gaping emptiness within this school system became. And the reason for this great emptiness was that the method of teaching stemmed from the old church schools, the Latin schools, whether directly transplanted into the modern *Gymnasium*[5] or adapted in some way. The old legalistic Latin method of teaching was still to be found in schools of all sorts. Combatting this and attempting partial reforms may have had historical significance, but did not release any forces of transformation.

So now we have the curriculum as it has been passed down to us, and we have the method. In what way were both of these presented to the children? Were there other assumptions, not purely instructional in character, that influenced the children's lives and destinies? All our schools are based on

5. A classical German secondary school that prepares its pupils for university study.

separation by social class. A lot has been said about comprehensive schools, but nothing was actually done in this direction until we founded the Waldorf School. This was done out
of the recognition that we were meant to take on a great social
mission.

Children coming to class on their very first day experienced
not only the crisis we have described as a soul and spiritual one,
but also a social crisis. On that day, children coming home
from primary school or from the *Gymnasium* and meeting their
playmates necessarily became aware of so-called class differ-
ences. From the very first day, they were fed this poison pro-
duced by the separation of the different classes of society. This
is the crisis in social feeling, in the child's naive feeling-life as a
whole, that confronted the child on the very first day.

What is the outcome of something like this? We can know
what modern spiritual science has worked out on the subject.
We can see that what develops into a formative force in teaching children around the age of seven can be effective and can
set itself certain tasks because at this point certain forces have
been set free in the child as a result of an organic development
that has already been completed. These are forces we can
work with. We can work with them in such a way that they
bring about the inner development and education of the
human being and leave their imprint on the further course of
organic development. Spiritual science, whose methods we
are trying to incorporate, supplies this basic way of looking at
the matter.

If we contrast this to old school practices, it must be said
that the old school had no connection to the forces that are
freed up organically and that come under consideration at this
stage of life. Thus it sinned in failing to acknowledge a view
such as this, which it would have had to discover if its instructional practices had been sound. On the one hand, because the

old school was not able to shape these freed-up forces, they began to run rampant, so that urges developed that were not guided into the developmental direction laid out for them. On the other hand, organic forces that should be freed up only much later, that wanted to become free only much later (if we understand the nature of the child), were pressed into service from the very first day of school.

This brought about what you can observe in the skeletal system. Inner support was weakened; the skeleton was weakened. Certain possibilities of standing upright in life were taken from the children because they were presented from the very first day with an education that addressed only their heads, that spoke only to their understanding. It could not or did not want to penetrate any deeper.

Facts such as these are often reflected in small symptoms. In this connection, it was interesting to find the statement in Haug's book that French, which we introduce in the first grade, as you know, should not be taught at that stage because it is an irrational language.

What is revealed in this characteristic statement? We can clearly see here that what is standing in front of the child is not a living person but a big fat book entitled *Grammar*, a fateful book for all of us. Grammar cannot be presented to children at this grade level; this is an impossibility tantamount to the impossibility for people with old-school habits of letting the living power of language play into the child's development. In the *Gymnasium*, this book stands there, and in the primary schools something else replaces the living personality who is actually meant to bring life's contents to the children. In the primary schools we have gotten away from the big book; instead, there are many more cards, charts and tables, all of which are supposed to be presented to the children so that they will learn to form judgments and conclusions.

If we understand the nature of the child correctly, we will be forced to admit that children have subtle reasons for not paying attention when they are confronted with a lesson of this sort. The power of wisdom that wants to protect them from harm makes them resist the big book, resist an intellectual way of looking at things. The inattentiveness that appears is a means of self-defense for them. They are evading the leveling influences of a lesson of this sort. If you teach like this from the first hour to the last, then the children attempt to escape from the lesson by being inattentive.

But how can this attempt possibly succeed in a school with any form of discipline? Not only is the material presented in the way described above, but the children are also expected to adjust to a different subject matter three or four times in the course of a morning, so they are thrown from one level to another. Those who know how to follow the school's development clearly realize that most recently the attempt was made to shorten the lessons still further, to 45 minutes each, to have the subject matter flow past in a movie-like fashion. This division was then extended to the individual lessons. How was that done? The formal stages of instruction established by Ziller are a masterpiece of modern methodology, and have been universally accepted in the primary schools.[6] Let me make it clear to you what a teacher of this sort has to accomplish in a single 45-minute lesson. The material is supposed to be presented to the children in six stages: First, the introduction. Second, consolidation. Third, enlivening the subject matter. Then comes the stage of making the subject accessible. This stage is not very

---

6. Tuiskon Ziller, 1817-1882, a student of Herbart and author of *Einleitung in die allgemeine Pädagogik* [An Introduction to General Pedagogy], published in 1856, and *Grundlegung zur Lehre vom erziehenden Unterricht* [Laying the Foundations for a Theory of Educational Instruction], published in 1865.

extensive. Then comes the stage of mastering the material, and last the stage of putting it to use, all in the same lesson. But this is repeated four times in the same morning in different subject areas.

You will have to admit that I am right in saying that *our* children cannot be dealt with according to this abusive method. But what happened when these mistreated children tried to evade the effects of the methodology and curriculum that required that on Tuesday, May 11, this particular goal must have been achieved in all classes at this grade level? What happened then?

This is where discipline came into effect. From the very first lesson, it worked with means that inevitably poisoned the children's entire moral life. Children who had been accustomed to expressing themselves freely and naturally found themselves confronted with praise or blame at every turn. Schematization set in. From the very beginning, the children adapted to the possibility of being called upon, so only in some cases did they participate attentively in the lesson. If they had been accustomed to expressing themselves freely and tried to do the same in school, they found themselves reprimanded and cut off whenever they tried to approach the teacher in this way, and had to be prepared for punishments that must have occasioned grave misgivings in their naive soul life. They then had to complete specific assignments rather than having the attitude awakened in them that it is a pleasure to be permitted to do schoolwork. Homework received the stamp of a punishment. The children got a very strange impression of lessons of this sort. Instruction as a whole had something to do with a system of punishment, and this was expressed in organic impairments that stunted their young growth and allowed certain things in them to grow rampant that would otherwise have unfolded in a healthy way.

I would like to point out that this is related to a very specific phenomenon that occurs in the later grades. Students
deal with the school system as a whole with a sarcasm that
pervades all of their behavior toward their teachers and their
schools. You all know from your own school days what fun it
was to be critical of the teachers. Add to that the phenomenon
of suicides among children of school age. These ominous phenomena are becoming ever more pronounced, and school
administrators are ever more helpless in the face of them. Real
life forces that want to become active in a natural and appropriate form of instruction have been dammed up. Everything
that has been held back in this way then causes the nervous-
ness that we see as a typical ailment of the times manifesting
in the school system.

Now let us ask ourselves what has been accomplished, what
has been brought to a conclusion of sorts, when grade school
has been completed. Our primary-school students leave school
in their fifteenth year. People who have had a lot to do with the
proletariat and who have often had to look working people in
the face will notice the phenomenon of a harshness of sorts
that leaves its mark on these people's faces. Much has been said
about this, but little thought has been given to it. It has not
been observed, however, that this is inevitable, an unavoidable
consequence of the fact that the life of feeling is set free in the
fourteenth year, and for the majority of our compatriots, their
education has been cut off at this point. How could anything
different come of it, if feeling abilities are not able to become
formative forces in these people's destiny?

Those who continued on were now seriously introduced to
the old Latin method I spoke about in the beginning. The
study of classical languages was emphasized more, or alterna-
tively the study of the sciences, which in a certain respect are
also only the heritage of the Roman Empire and of Roman law.

The consequence of this was that if people leaving primary school had inevitably been restricted in their development, the people leaving the humanistic *Gymnasium* were supposed to represent the ideal of humanistic education. Being able to speak languages that were studied for their own sake was regarded as an accomplishment. People failed to notice, however, that being preoccupied with such languages reflected back on the entire being of the person in question, and that people who had spent many hours in the study of ancient Greek had become incapable of understanding the language of everyday facts. And the people coming out of the *Realschule*[7] later became the practitioners of *Realpolitik*, always insisting on facts and on laws of all sorts, but failing to see that reality is influenced by trends totally different from the ones they call their laws.

Keeping this in mind, we can see the fateful consequences of graduating from all three of these types of schools—forces were held back that could have worked to form organs, influencing education in the deepest sense of the word,[8] while on the other hand forces that were not able to flow in had to run rampant. If left uncultivated, the life of feeling has the tendency to fall into sentimentality at every turn.

And what happened to the will? Either it was so broken that we now have human wrecks serving in responsible positions, or on the other hand we have those brutal and violent human beings who come out trampling everything under their feet as a consequence of not having been able to cultivate their will.

These phenomena have been frequently summed up and abundantly criticized. During the revolutionary period, the

---

7. A modern secondary school emphasizing modern languages, mathematics and science.
8. Translator's note: there is a play on words in the German here— "forming" and "education" are the same word, "Bildung."

opinion arose that now, out of the foul-smelling vapor of new forces brewing, something like a new stream of life would be able to flow into the school system as such; it would be possible to whip up criticism to the point of doing something constructive. Since then we have not grown tired of using the term "comprehensive school" over and over again to label efforts that thought to get in touch with the times. But when we look at the legislature's omissions, we will not be able to avoid seeing the great danger that confronts us. Although the traditional structure of the schools has been changed outwardly, we see that because of the desire to expand the so-called "school franchise," the danger is imminent. We are seeing that primary schools can turn into denominational schools, party schools, or schools of specific economic groups. Even less thought than before is being given to the universal human aspect, and this is now happening at the insistence of a legally functioning bureaucratic apparatus.

You will find that the relevance of bureaucrats has not been reduced under recent conditions. On the contrary, they are able to have a much greater effect and to subvert much more than they could under the old system. Just observe how jealously they make sure that all regulations are observed. In the face of this brutal will, we will not be able to avoid the conclusion that it will not be easily possible to realize our educational ideal. We must be prepared for the possibility that the instructional content we are supposed to bring to the children will be regulated to an even greater extent than it was previously, especially in the subject of history.

What will the further consequence of this be? The result will be that the bureaucratic character of teaching will become even more pronounced.

All of this stands in contrast to our world of today, to the needs of our times, which are asking for something totally different from the pale glimmer of things to come that people want to spread over the school system and beyond it. Why is it impossible for existing innovations to lead to that goal? Here we come upon a very strange law: If something is conceived of somewhere and it is not able to pour itself out fully into the object of its concern because people are not putting all their energy into it, its effect is not to decrease the negative circumstances, but to unite with them. Beneath the surface, it flows over to join them. Lichtwark put it like this: "Partial reforms accomplish only an intensification of existing tendencies."[9] What we must expect in this case is anything but a restructuring. We can only expect a further intensification of efforts that are already present.

Now, I have spread out this picture before you to clarify something that does not seem exaggerated to me, something that many teachers would like to see eliminated from their lives and destinies, because if we want to have the efforts of our independent school flow into the public life of our times in the right way, we must know the danger that threatens us from the old school system. It cannot be the task of my remarks today to describe these efforts again.

Even if the prescriptions that legally regulated the old school system are lacking in our school, that does not mean that we have made our task any easier. In fact, we have made it more difficult. Our times require us to take up heavy burdens for the sake of the evolution on which we base our hopes for the future. Having taken up these heavy burdens, we will be able to carry them only with the help of all those who have lent us their confidence. They must be aware that the smallest results are of significance; they must follow the progress of our life in the school with great seriousness. Not a single lesson, not a single other

---

9. Alfred Lichtwark, 1852–1914, art educator.

undertaking that belongs to the school, is envisaged in the way in which it would result from old educational practices.

What is being accomplished here is a life-force for our nation itself. It is a force whose effects we need. Our times are thirsting for them. We must bring about a totally different encounter between home and school than was the case under the old school practices. Either there was a conflict, or the children were thrown back and forth between home and school, so to speak. We often encounter the opinion that parents are happy once the children are in school; they want them to be in school all day long and are very upset by "unreasonable" demands that they should support the activity of the school. In a very subtle way, children pick up on all the nuances that are circulated in their environment. When the children can observe that their parents look at things in ways that differ from what is said in school, the children get involved in a conflict, and it becomes impossible to focus on the children to the intended effect.

Now that we have brought our school into existence, now that we have worked with all our might to realize a part of it, the old educational practices are still alive, and people who grew up under them are trying to introduce old requirements into this new thing. They would like to judge the whole thing according to a compartmentalized standard. It can happen that people are concerned when our school, which tries to develop *all* of a child's forces, cannot show why a child has not yet learned this or that. They are very concerned about it. We must take into account that these concerns are not justified, or we would not be able to speak of a new school, but would simply have taken up old educational practices and repackaged them in some way. What deviates from the old practices in the Waldorf School is done out of educational practices that do not flow out of clever, rationally thought-out ways of looking at things.

Rather, it flows out of forces that are related to the developmental forces of young people and of our nation as a whole. Having assured you of this, we hope that you will feel sufficiently connected to what we are doing to grant us your confidence. You must have patience and wait for this to bear fruit.

Meanwhile, the mood that ensouls and enlivens all our children can be taken as an indication of what the fruit will be. They bring it to school with them; they realize that learning is not a punishment here. Take this mood, which is even evident in the fresh red cheeks of some of our pupils, as a sign that things are coming to fruition. Do not let yourselves be intimidated by the ghosts trying to take our declining times by storm. Tell yourselves that on stepping out into life as a mature person, a child who has grown up here shall be compared only to him or herself.

When we apply this way of looking at things to the school, the creative joy that enlivens us will bear fruit, and we will see that contemporary life is forced to take the school into account. Creative forces can only come out of schools in which such forces are not held back but are developed, so that the children's first day of school does not constitute a crisis. Instead, the children are introduced to school in a way that opens them up to their life to come. They leave school, not as violent individuals and not as people burdened merely with head-knowledge, but as individuals who can stand for an education of a new sort, the truly human education of a new age. Inherent in truly understanding the human being is a pledge to support our nation's evolution in the future.

This task, too, is great, but harshness is a sign of our times. People do not want to see the face of our times so clearly that its embittered lines are visible. They want to avoid seeing it, to draw veil upon veil over this face because they are afraid of what it might say. The tasks that we have taken on are great and severe.

But we believe that there can be people who love these tasks doubly because of their very greatness and severity. We unite with you in the hope that you will learn to love them for this. Something new and fresh will be able to come from this severity.

What we have to stand for is harsh and severe, but this severity will give those of us who work out of the Independent Waldorf School the strength to inscribe a fiery sign on the brow of our declining age. May this school, as it lives out its life among hollow phrases, find the strength to die a mighty death so that the sun of the day to come may shine on it.

Address at the assembly
at the end of the first school year

July 24, 1920

My dear children! Today, now that we are at the end of our first school year here in our dear Waldorf School, let us inscribe on our souls something of why we are actually in this school. What does it mean that our dear friend Herr Molt, together with Frau Molt, founded this Waldorf School for you, my dear children, and for humankind? What does it mean that you come here every morning in order to learn something good? What does it mean, above all, that there are people who are taking great pains to guide you into life so that you will grow up to be good and capable people?

You know, my dear children, that I have often come here during this school year, and in each class I always asked you a question, a question that comes straight from my heart. I often asked you, "Do you love your teachers?" ["Yes!" shout the children.] And you know, you always answered me as warmly as you just did today.

Now there will be weeks in which you do not see your teachers for a while, and so now I want to say something different to you. I hope your hearts will often answer this question during vacation. Now I would like to say to you, "Now that you are not going to see your teachers, learn to be grateful to them." In the same way that you have learned, tried hard to learn to love your teachers, now learn to feel firmly in your heart that you are grateful to your teachers, so that when you ask yourselves, "Am I grateful to my teachers?" you can honestly and heartily say, "Yes, I am grateful."

Now there is something else I want to say to you. You see, my dear children, here with us it should not happen that as Waldorf School students you say, "Hey, school is over now; it's vacation. When we're in school, we have to work hard and learn, but now we can be lazy. We don't have to do anything. We're glad that we can be lazy." You know that is not what we want to say. We should say something else; we should say, "Yes, it's a beautiful day. During the day we experience many beautiful things along with some that are sad and painful, but what would human beings be if they could not experience through their senses everything that divine spirituality has put into the world, everything that is so great and beautiful and true."

But unless we can also sleep and rest, we cannot use our ears and eyes properly to hear and see all the beautiful things divine spirituality has put into the world. Think about how after enjoying the day, you have to rest at night, and then in the morning you are strengthened again. Your eyes see better and your ears hear better. If you had to stay awake all the time, you would surely not be able to enjoy and learn about life in all its truth and beauty the way divine spirituality made it.

This is also how it is in life as a whole. You should not think, "Now that it's vacation we can be lazy;" you should think, "All of what we received from our dear teachers, everything that humankind has learned so that individuals can know it—we received all this, and now we need a little rest, so that when we have rested, we can go back into our classes and be fresher and more lively. In fact, we will each go into the next grade; with new forces we will once again take into our hearts what our teachers will give us through their love and hard work, what humanity has learned in service to humanity." This is how we should think of it—that we are resting during the vacation to get strong again for the whole new school year.

Then, my dear children, I would like to tell you a little about what it means that this Waldorf School of ours exists, and what it means that we are here in this school. You see, the person you are going to grow up to be, this person has a physical body, a soul and a spirit. You each have a body, a soul, and a spirit. And when a person is very little and is born into the world, this body and soul and spirit are all very incomplete. In you, they are still incomplete, but they are supposed to become more complete. Here in the Waldorf School your body will be shaped to become skilled at everything a person has to do in life. Your teachers have worked hard at this on your behalf; you have been introduced to eurythmy, for example, which works to make your body very skillful in life, and many other things have been brought to you so that you will become people who are skillful and capable and strong in their bodies. When you are small, you are fairly clumsy. You have to become more skill-ful. It is the same with the soul which is in each one of you. But it has to be developed so that it can send out threads in all directions for life. This is like unwinding the strands from a tangled ball of yarn—the threads for your life have to be untangled from your soul. This is how the soul develops, and this happens for you so that you become good and capable with regard to your forces for life. Good strong forces for life have to be fetched up out of your souls. And your spirit—yes, my dear children, if we did not educate the spirit, we would not be human beings at all. The spirit must be educated so that we become very good and capable human beings.

Now you see, when a person has worked all day or when a child has played and learned well and then sleeps, sometimes dreams come to them from their sleep. Most of you have experienced dreams. Sometimes they are very beautiful dreams, sometimes ugly dreams. And now you are going to go rest during vacation. Then something will come to you that can be compared to a dream. You see, during vacation, when you think back to when you were in school, it may be that you think, "Oh, I had nice teachers, I learned a lot, I was glad to be able to go to school." And when you think that, those are beautiful dreams during your vacation. And when you think, "Oh, I should have been less lazy; I didn't like to go to school," and so forth, then you are having bad dreams during vacation. Think back often during this vacation to when you were in school; for example, think like this: "My thoughts are drawn back to the Waldorf School, where my body is shaped for skillful activity, where my soul is developed to be strong in life, where my spirit develops so that I can be truly human." When you think often like this about how your body is being shaped, your soul developed and your spirit educated, you will send yourself a good dream for your time of rest, and then your vacation time will also contribute something to making you a good and capable person in life.

You know, when I came in today, one of your good little fellow students gave me something. Let's see what it is. Look, this is what he gave me—a washcloth and a flower! Now I guess I must wash myself and dry my hands, and perhaps the flower is meant to say that your lessons are something that blooms as beautifully as this nice little white flower. [Rudolf Steiner holds up the washcloth.] And perhaps this could remind us that what we learn here is also something we can use to wash away everything in our souls that is incomplete, all bad thoughts and feelings that want to make us be lazy and not pay attention. I would like to give you each a little spiritual cloth so you can wash away all the laziness and lack of hard work and inattentiveness, and so on. So I am very glad that you have given me this little symbol and that I can show you how to use it to wash away a whole lot of what should not be in your souls.

And look at this little flower! You have learned many things here that you needed to learn, and what you learned is so many little flowers like this in your soul. Think about this when you remind yourselves that your thoughts are hurrying back to the Waldorf School where your bodies are trained to be skillful, your soul is developed to be strong for life, and your spirit unfolds so that you can be properly human—and think about how flowers like this are being cultivated in your soul day after day, and how grateful you should be for that. Everything in life can be of service to us and help us think about what is right. That, dear children, is what I wanted to say to you.

Think about each other, too! You have gotten to know each other and also, I hope, learned to love each other. Think about each other very, very often, and think about how good it was that you came together so that your teachers could help you grow into good and capable people. Don't think, "Now we can be lazy," but think, "We need to rest, and when we have rested we will come back and be fresh and ready to receive what our dear teachers bring to us."

And now, although you will not yet be able to understand it, I would like to say a few words in your presence to your dear teachers, who have now put all the diligent work of the

Waldorf School behind them, and I would like to shake their hands. First of all, I would like to shake hands with Herr Molt and Frau Molt for having created this Waldorf School for us so that we can try to do something for humanity in its dire straits. My dear friends—as I said, I am speaking to the teachers, but you children can also hear it and can remember it later—the years behind us have been bitter ones for humanity, years in which people beat and bloodied and shot each other. There are still other bitter things in front of us, for the times still look very bad. But then the Waldorf teachers were the first to find the courage to appear here and to start to believe something that I am convinced that people today must start to believe above all else. The Waldorf teachers came here and said, "Yes, we have to work on the children so that when we are old, something will have happened to the children that can prevent unhappiness and bitterness of this sort from overcoming people." This requires a certain courage and it requires hard work, but above all it requires something that awakens in human hearts the possibility of not sleeping, but of staying awake. That, dear Waldorf teachers, is why I want to shake your hands so warmly. If many people would wake up and look at the decision you have come to instead of sleeping through it, if what happens here would find successors, then you would realize that you were the first to work at something that is so very necessary for our future as human beings.

Dear children, when your teachers came into school each morning, they were people who clearly grasped the task of our times and devoted themselves diligently to what was required of them. And it was always a warm moment for me when I asked you, "Do you love your teachers?" and you so heartily answered, "Yes!" During the vacation I will also wonder whether you are grateful to your teachers. But you, dear Waldorf teachers, let me warmly shake your hands. I thank you in the name of the spirit of humanity which we are trying to cultivate throughout our spiritual movement. In this spirit, I shake your hands for everything you have accomplished on behalf of the future ideals of humanity. Today is the day for us to be able to remember these things, and it is the day when you children should feel how grateful you ought to be to these teachers of yours.

There is still something I would like to say today. Alongside everything we have learned here, which the individual teachers have demonstrated so beautifully, there is something else present, something that I would like to call the spirit of the Waldorf School. It is meant to lead us to true piety again. Basically, it is the spirit of Christianity that wafts through all our rooms, that comes from every teacher and goes out to every child, even when it seems that something very far from religion is being taught, such as arithmetic, for example. Here it is always the spirit of Christ that comes from the teacher and is to enter the hearts of the children—this spirit that is imbued with love, real human love. This is why I want you children to feel that not only have you learned something here, you have also gradually learned to feel what it is for one person to love another. And so now as you are going on vacation, I would like you to think of all your schoolmates with a warm-hearted "Until we meet again! Until we meet again, when we come back strengthened into these rooms, when we can once again work with our teachers on what will make us into good and capable people."

You see, dear children, you must consider how life here in this school is connected to the whole of human life. When people get old, they are seventy or eighty years old. Life brings joy and sorrow, beauty and ugliness. When we get old, we are seventy or eighty, as I said. We can compare our life to a day with twenty-four hours. If this day represents our life, then a year that we spend in this day of life would be about twenty minutes long, and your eight years in primary school would be something like two to three hours out of your whole life. So the time that you spend in the Waldorf School makes up two or three hours out of your whole life. And when we go through the other twenty hours we have for living, for working, for becoming aware of the spirit, for doing things with other people so that something good can happen in the world—when we go through these hours, it can be a real comfort for our hearts, a real strength for our lives, if we are able to realize that the two or three hours of life we spent in primary school gave us something for our whole life, gave us strength and spirit and the ability to work.

Let us say this to ourselves, my dear children, now on this last day of our first school year in the Waldorf School, but during the vacation, let us remember something else again and again. I would like to write it in your souls so that it blooms there like this cute little flower, so that you think of it often: "Let my thoughts hurry back to my dear Waldorf School, where my body is trained to work and to do good, where my soul is developed to be strong for life, where my spirit is awakened to be truly good and human." We want you all to become such good and capable people someday, when you are grown up and out there in life.

I wanted to speak to you from heart to heart today. I wanted to say this to you out of love, and I say it to you so that you can take note of it. Once again, think of your thoughts hurrying back to your dear Waldorf School, where your body is shaped to work capably in life, where your soul is developed for strength in life, where your spirit is awakened to true humanity. That is how it should be. And so now we will leave each other, and when we come back, we will go on as we have done before.

Afterwards you will receive your reports.[10] Whoever gets a good report should not take it as an indication that it is now all right to be lazy, and whoever gets a bad report need not immediately start to cry, but should think about trying harder next year.

Out of the spirit of the Waldorf School, shake your teachers' hands and say to each other, "We will be back in fall to learn to do good work, to develop our souls to be strong for life, and to awaken our spirit to true humanity."

And so, until we meet again!

- -

Address at a monthly assembly

November 23, 1920

I have come to you once again from the country with the high mountains; Herr Molt picked me up in Dornach, where our building is going up, so I could come see you.

We are working very hard in Switzerland and have no time to climb the beautiful mountains your dear teachers have described so nicely for you. We have no time to climb up there and look at the sun, but it is something like sunlight for us if we can come to Stuttgart now and then, because we love this hill here. It is certainly easier to climb than the Swiss mountains, but the pleasure we get in climbing up this hill to our dear Waldorf School is a spiritual pleasure more than anything else. It is a spiritual pleasure for us because this is where you,

---

10. At the end of the school year, instead of receiving grades, the children received brief characterizations of their behavior and of how they worked.

dear children of the Waldorf School, are taught to become good and capable people for life.

It has always been a joy to my heart to spend a lot of time in Stuttgart in our dear Waldorf School. This time, I am sorry to say that I will have less time because other work kept me away. However, I hope to be able to be with you at least for a little while in the next few days. I especially wanted to greet you warmly today, since this assembly falls in the time of Advent and the wonderful festival of Christmas.

Once again, I would like to greet your dear teachers, who are very concerned about how to teach you to be good and capable human beings. But if you work hard out of love for your teachers and follow their directions, then all their concerns will fall away and be replaced with joy in their hearts, joy at being able to teach you children, who have been sent to them from the spiritual world, to be really good and capable people for the future.

Now that I have been able to greet your teachers, I would like to greet you, too. The first impression I got of you was that you were yelling and being really noisy. I thought you really could be a little less noisy. But we have to look at the bright side of things: While you are being so noisy, you are not having useless thoughts. You should not be cooking up useless thoughts even when you are not yelling. But I hope that when I see you in your classes, you will not be yelling like that. There are also times when children must behave differently and not sound like so many chirping birds.

Now there is one thing I always have to tell you: You are meant to grow up to be good and capable people. However, you can become good and capable people only by trying to cultivate three qualities in yourselves and thinking about them again and again. What you take in here in school must last you for the rest of your life, but it will be able to stay in your memory, to stay in you as a strength for life, only if you pay attention in your classes, if you pay attention to the good men and women who are your teachers. Paying attention will make what you learn in childhood carry over into your later years of life. What your teachers say to you comes from incredibly hard work on their part, from the strength of their devotion and from their love for you. But what comes from their love must also be able to get to you, and that is why I always say the same thing to you: Love your teachers, because love will carry what comes from your teachers' hearts into your hearts and into your heads. Love is the best way for what teachers have to give to flow into their students. That is why I am going to ask you again today, "Do you love your teachers? Do you still love them?" [The children shout, "Yes!"] That is the second thing—to love your teachers. The third thing is hard work. Nothing can be accomplished without hard work. You must work hard, and then what you have learned by loving your teachers will become a real strength for your life.

When you are trying to cultivate these three qualities, you must develop the right feeling. You are now approaching the time of year when the spirit who became the spirit of love came down from distant worlds. Now, when the festival of Christ is approaching, think of the many beautiful words the Christ spoke. Among them are the words, "I shall be with you always, until the earth no longer exists."[11]

Thus the spirit of Christ is always with us. Each Christmas and each Easter shows us how to turn our thoughts to how the spirit of Christ is among us. This spirit of Christ is also your teachers' great teacher. Through your teachers, the spirit of Christ works into your hearts.

Cultivate everything your dear teachers accomplish through their work, everything they bring to you out of deep concern for

---

11. Free paraphrase of the words of Matthew 28:20.

you. Cultivate this through the three qualities of paying attention, love for your teachers, and hard work, and then what you
carry from your young years into your later years will be just
what humanity needs—the strength of human work. You will
grow up to be good and capable human beings. That is what
you are meant to become through the Waldorf School. Do it by
paying attention, loving your teachers, and working hard!

Address and discussion at a parents' evening[1]

January 13, 1921

Dear friends; dear ladies and gentlemen! You have chosen to entrust your children's education to the Waldorf School, which has now been in existence for more than a year. If we want to communicate the Waldorf School's methods and manner of instruction in a few indications—we do not have time for more than that tonight—it is best to start by mentioning one thing that we need in the Waldorf School much more than in any other school. In this school more that in any other, we need to work with the parents in a relationship of trust if we want to move forward in the right way. Our teachers absolutely depend on finding this relationship of trust with the children's parents, since our school is fundamentally based on spiritual freedom—by which I do not mean, of course, any phantasmagorical spiritual license on the part of the children. Our school takes its place in our overall culture as an independent school in the best sense of the word. Just think about the otherwise compulsory integration of school life into public life by the civil authorities. Schools have been conceived wholly in the context of the state establishment which they are intended

---

1. The wording of this speech and of the discussion that follows was revised by Rudolf Steiner himself for publication in the *Mitteilungsblatt für die Mitglieder des Vereins Freie Waldorfschule* [Newsletter for Members of the Independent Waldorf School Association], March 1922, Vol. 2.

to serve exclusively, supplying the state with human beings of the sort it requires. That this is not also in the interest of truly healthy individual development is the recognition on which the Waldorf School is founded. The Waldorf School is intended to serve healthy human development above all else. All the instruction and education taking place in the Waldorf School are to be built up on the basis of healthy human development.

As you know, people today often say that a child's individuality should be developed in school, that children should not be force-fed, that we should draw out what is present in each child. This is a very nice principle. There are many, many equally nice principles in the pedagogical literature of the nineteenth and twentieth centuries. In an abstract respect, this pedagogical literature, which is supposed to teach teachers how to teach, is not bad at all. An extraordinary number of good things have been said about education by all kinds of humanitarian people, but we cannot say that these good intentions correspond in all instances to the actual practice of education, as we may call it. And that is what it all depends on for us in the Waldorf School—on building up a real, true practice of education. And I actually do believe that it will be possible to arrive at a true practice of education through cultivating the spiritual life that takes place in our circles in particular, for this is especially intended to enable us to understand the human being better than any other way of cultivating the spiritual life could do. And this applies not only to the adult human being, but also to the child, to the human being in the becoming.

People often believe that they understand growing human beings in the right way. And at least as a general rule—and in fact this is much more often the case than those who are not closely involved with children believe—there is indeed a human relationship in which a very good understanding of the developing human being is present, and that is the relationship of a father or mother to the child. The relationship of a father and mother to their child is a natural one. It is one in which they grow into living with the child, and they have a certain feeling for the right thing to do. Of course they may also do the wrong thing at times, but that is because of more or less unnatural circumstances, because of an unnatural development in their proper fatherly or motherly feeling.

However, when the child grows up and enters the time when the change of teeth begins, then what home can be for the child is no longer enough. If this were not the case, then we would not need to have schools. But at this point the child must go to school, and then the important thing is for the child to receive an education that can guide him or her as a developing individual toward life, consciously and out of an understanding of the nature of the child. In order for this to take place, however, a real understanding of the human being must be alive in the child's teacher. And a real understanding of the human being actually requires the teacher to be active in the noblest of the sciences, the science of the soul. Because the human being is fashioned out of the entire world, a real knowledge of the human being requires us to look into the whole world with a free and penetrating gaze. Someone who is not sufficiently warmly interested in knowing about the world to focus on it will also not be capable of insight into the human heart and mind, and especially not into the aspect of this that is meant to make a child develop into a complete human being. Anyone who is incapable of feeling everything that exists in the world as the physical element, everything that pervades and governs the world as the soul element, and everything that is contained in it as the spiritual element, will not be able to understand the nature of the child, because there is still present in the child something of the mysterious working of what is brought along when a human being descends from quite different worlds, from spiritual worlds, to the parents from whom he or she takes on a body.

When we observe a child in the first years of life, from week to week and from month to month, it is really the most wonderful thing in the world's becoming. The world's most wonderful secrets are revealed when we observe how something that is at first indefinite grows out spiritually through the child's physical being, how indeterminate features that still bear traces of the merely natural are shaped by the inner element of spirit and soul, how the soul gradually works its way out through the eyes that gaze into life with ever-increasing understanding. It is wonderful to see how children become one with their surroundings, how they recreate almost everything they see there in all that they do in their still clumsy fashion, and how they finally grow together with their surroundings in learning to speak. The first seven years of their life are totally dedicated to growing together with their surroundings in this way. When the children are admitted to school, around the time when they are approaching the change of teeth, then everything we undertake with them must be based on this knowledge of the human being.

However, there is also something else on which it must be based. We may believe that we understand the nature of the growing human being. However, what induces a child to read, write, and do arithmetic must be drawn from the very nature of the growing person, and here we soon notice what a complicated thing it is to truly understand the human being. In our teacher-training courses we may have learned methodically and well how to teach reading and writing and so forth. Then we can make an effort to apply what we learned there, and in practical terms we can even do very well up to a certain point, and yet we achieve nothing in our teaching unless a certain relationship exists between teacher and child, a relationship of real mutual love. That is what we really try to cultivate in our Waldorf School as something that is pedagogically and methodologically just as necessary as mere outer skill. We want an atmosphere of love to be alive in every class, and for instruction to take place on the basis of this atmosphere of love.

But this love cannot be mandated. It is not accomplished by giving sermons on this type of love in teacher-training institutes. Love cannot be taught just like that. But as teachers, we actually need more love than we need for the other aspects of our lives. You see, the amount of love people usually have for their children, no matter how many they may have, is small compared to what a teacher needs. No one has as many children of their own as a teacher usually has to teach in a class. As adults we develop the love of a man for a woman and a woman for a man, and this is also something that is meant to be kept within a narrow circle, because it is not good if love of this sort is divided up among too many personalities. So the love that flows from an individual out into life is always meant to be distributed among relatively few people. Of course we are supposed to love all human beings, but that is kept within certain limits. To include the millions is only possible to a certain extent.

However, it is absolutely necessary for a teacher to have the same degree of love, although possibly in a somewhat different way, for the children in his or her class that parents have for their children or a man for the woman he loves or a woman for the man she loves. It must be the same love and just as intense. It is transferred more to a soul and spiritual level, but it must be present. We are not born with this love; we must acquire it from elsewhere, from a science, from knowledge. This science, however, is not as dry and abstract as today's natural sciences or scientific activity in general, whose dryness and solemnity have rubbed off on education. We can have love of this sort only as a result of a science that truly deals with the spirit and reveals the spirit, for where a science provides spirit, it also provides love. Thus the cultivation of the spiritual life, the spiritual science, that has led to founding the Waldorf School provides the teachers with this real love. We need this love; everything must be based on it. Even the school's most matter-of-course methods must be based on it. Above all else, the spirit of understanding the world and the spirit of love must be present in instruction as it is practiced in the Waldorf School, in the education that we want to provide. And this cannot be accomplished with cliches and generalities. It can be accomplished only if we know how to apply in detail and over and over again what we know about the development of the child from month to month and from year to year.

In ordinary education, people nowadays immediately begin to present the child with something that paralyzes the individual's entire healthy development. Let us look back on the development of humanity for a moment. There have been times— and we cannot be so arrogant as to imagine that people in those times were stupid and childish—when people did not yet learn to read and write in the modern sense. At most, they learned a primitive form of arithmetic. Today we learn to read and write, but we do not learn reading and writing as they first developed out of nonreading and nonwriting; we learn something that has become very rational and conventionalized. When we do not hesitate to teach children the reading and writing that are now customary in our dealings with each other, we are basically using very artificial means to introduce them to something that is foreign to them. When children come to us in the first grade, we must be careful not to force-feed them with what adults are supposed to be able to do. And now I am going to speak of something that our dear friend Herr Molt already pointed to—that in the Waldorf School children learn to read and write somewhat later than in other schools. There are good reasons for this. In many respects, it is a mistake to learn to read and write as early as this happens in other schools. The point is not to make the children acquire certain capabilities as quickly as possible, but rather to teach them to be good and capable people later on in life, people who do not make life difficult for themselves. Outer circumstances can make life difficult enough for many people as it is; we do not need an inner feeling of weakness or inability messing up our lives. We must find a method of teaching reading and writing very carefully and on the basis of the children's natural tendencies and skills.

Let me just mention that we start by first letting the children draw certain forms from which the forms contained in the letters of the alphabet are developed. We let the children get into reading by starting with writing, because the more we start from something that has its basis in the entire human being, the better it is for the children's development. In reading and writing as we adults use them to interact with each other or to learn about things belonging to spiritual or other aspects of life, the signs for letters, the signs constituting our words, have become something very conventionalized. Ancient peoples still used a pictorial script that contained something concrete. There was still a connection between what was used to express something in writing and what was being expressed. In our letters, however, it is no longer possible to recognize anything of what is being expressed. Thus if we simply teach children these letters as the end result of a long process of development, we are forcing them into something that is foreign to them. Instead, we must lead the children in a sensible way from things they enjoy drawing, from something that comes from their whole being, to the shapes of the letters. Only afterwards can we develop reading on the basis of this.

I have tried to use this example to show you the thrust of our art of education—to really read in growing human beings what we are meant to do with them. Those who understand human nature are well aware of how things are connected in life. We often do not observe much of what is most important in life. We often find people—and today they are much more numerous than we believe—who take no real pleasure in anything, who tire very easily, and who grow old before their time—at least inwardly with regard to their souls—and so on. We are not clear as to the origin of this. It comes from the fact that as children in the sixth, seventh and eighth years of life, they were not taught writing and reading in the right way. Those who understand human nature know that children who learned to read in the right way, who were not force-fed at age six or seven but learned to read and write naturally, may master reading and writing a bit later, but they will take along what they gained from learning to read and write as a real gift that they will have for the rest of their lives.

If we drum it into them in all kinds of artificial ways that disregard their natural tendencies and developmental possibilities, we can get children to read and write at seven-and-a-half, but in many respects we will have crippled these children's souls for life. In contrast, if we have gone about it in the right way, the children only learn to read and write at age eight, but life forces develop in them as they are learning. That is what we want. While the children are in school, we want them to acquire life forces, forces with effects that will last for their entire lives.

As inhabitants of Central Europe, you do not need to be told that we find ourselves in a terrible situation today. The misery and suffering are truly not becoming any less, but are increasing almost from day to day. And it can be said that much of this stems simply from the fact that people can no longer find their way into life in the right way; they can no longer adapt to life. To be sure, the most important time with regard to people finding their way into life is not their school years, but a much later time, the time when they are in their twenties, between the ages of twenty and thirty. This is the time that earlier ages (which we cannot and do not want to wish back) called the transition from apprenticeship to mastery. There is sometimes something extremely sensible in the designation of such transitions.

This is the time in which people actually fully grow up. They must then find a way to become skillful in life. Then something happens that I would like to compare to the following image taken from nature. Let me remind you of a certain river that flows through Carinthia and Krain. As it flows from its source, it is known as the Poik. Then it disappears into a hole and is no longer visible. After a time it comes to the surface again. It is the same river; it has simply flowed underground for a while, but now as it continues above ground, it is called the Unz. Then it again disappears and flows underground. When it surfaces again, it is known as the Laibach. It surfaces again and again; it is the same water, but sometimes it flows underground.

It is also like this in a human life. There is something present in human life in the second, third, fourth, fifth, sixth, and seventh years of life, and also during the school years, in the form of children's urge to play. Everything that belongs to children's play is especially active at this age. Then, like the river, it sinks below the surface of human life. Later, when sexual maturity arrives and other things happen, we see that this urge to play is no longer active in the same way. But when people enter their twenties, the same thing that was present in play surfaces again. However, it no longer functions as the urge to play; it is now something different. It has now become the way in which the individual can find his or her way into life. And in fact, if children are allowed to play in the right way according to their particular potentials, when they are introduced to the right games, then they will be able to adapt to life in the right way. But if we miss out on something about the nature of the child in the games we introduce, the children will also lack skill in finding their place in life. This is how these things are related: The urge to play, the particular way in which a child plays, disappears and sinks below the surface of life. Then it resurfaces, but as something different, as the skill to adapt to life. There is an inner coherence in life throughout all its stages. We need to know this in order to teach children in the right way.

For example, there is a very important point in time in the life of a child that may sometimes come a bit earlier, sometimes a bit later, but always falls approximately between the ninth and tenth years of life. At this point in a person's life, a lot depends on having the right feeling of admiration and respect for one's teacher. Of course, this feeling should also be present at other times, but at this moment in life something essential is being decided for the child. It is really of extraordinarily great significance. That is why the art of education is so difficult to achieve—it rests on a thorough understanding of the human being. Many things that show up at later stages of life and cause a great deal of unhappiness, preventing people from finding their place in life and making them incapable of working, even causing them to develop tendencies toward physical illnesses, all stem from the fact that as children they were not dealt with in the right way between their ninth and tenth years of life. We do not believe this today, but it really is so. Until the ninth or tenth year of life, we must try to keep the children occupied with instructional material that does not force them to think about themselves too much. Instead, they should be thinking about things that are out there in life. Then, between the ninth and tenth years of life, we must begin to present them with concepts and images of plants and animals that help them make a transition from thinking about the world to thinking about themselves. All of our teaching must be designed to introduce things at the right moment, when the inner nature of the child requires it, so to speak.

What I am indicating to you in just a few words is actually a highly developed study of the human being on the basis of spiritual science. This is what makes it possible to develop a real art of education. This art of education, based on a truly spiritual scientific understanding of the human being, is meant to govern the entire Waldorf School; it is meant to be the spirit that prevails there. And in fact, we believe that much of what is so painful in our day and age is crying out for the next generation to be made good and capable through an education of this sort. We also believe that if parents understand why they are entrusting their children to a school that is set up on the basis of a real and thorough understanding of the human being, they also really understand what our present times demand. What we need in this school comes about through a relationship of this sort between the parents and the school. This is a part of how we work. If the children who come to school in the morning are sent off by parents who understand the school and therefore have the right kind of love for it, then the children will also be able to have the right experience of what is meant to come to meet them, more than anything else, when they open the door to the school and meet their teachers with the love that is the only source of truly appropriate instruction and education.

When what we introduce is presented at the right moment and lies within the children's abilities and potentials, it becomes a source of revitalization for the children for their entire lives. And when the parents of our children realize that we are actually working to produce people who will be both fit for and able to question a life that will become ever more difficult in decades to come, these parents will relate to the school in the right way. Our work must rest on the understanding of the parents. We cannot work in the same way as other schools that are protected by the state and by authorities of all sorts. We can only work only if we are met by an understanding community of parents. We are aware of what we are being given in the children in this school, whom we are trying to educate out of a true understanding of the human being and of what subjects can be employed at any given time. This is the awareness out of which our teachers can teach best. If, out of this awareness, we always try to give these children the best that can be given to them, then we need to have this school surrounded by a wall of parental understanding like the walls of a fortress. We love our children here; we teach on a basis of understanding the human being and of loving children, while around us a different love grows up, the parents' love for the being of our school. Given the lack of understanding and questionable moral development that we face today, it is only within this community that we are really able to work toward a future in which human beings will thrive.

The work that is to be done in this direction may be limited to a small community, but much can come out of this small community if it always meets the school with the right understanding.

Our teachers need an awareness of this sort because they lack all the compulsory disciplinary measures that teachers in other schools have to back them up, as it were. But nothing reasonable will ever happen in human life as a result of coercion. In order to be able to work in freedom, we need the parents to understand how we try to do this. And the fact that a very considerable number of people have been found who are sending their children to the Waldorf School demonstrates that at least a start has been made toward this understanding. We would like it to spread more and more, of course; we would like more and more people to realize that something good can come about only through a real, true art of education. But especially on evenings like tonight, we must be glad that we can come together in the spirit of wanting to bring about a better future for humanity by working together with those who are trying to raise and educate the generations to come in the sense of real knowledge of and love for the human being.

Of course it is not possible, even with the best of will, to fully achieve the ideal that hovers before us on our first attempt; something, however, has been achieved. To begin with, too, what we are doing will not meet with a full and thorough understanding. It is possible that many things will be misunderstood. Under certain circumstances, it will be possible for people to say, "Well, in this school some children are not being hit often enough. There are surely some children who need to be hit, either literally or figuratively." Such things are sometimes said, but not out of a thorough understanding of, or love for, the human being. There are methods that may work more slowly, but are more certain to develop the good in a person than any unnatural compulsory disciplinary measures. An understanding of some of these things can be achieved only gradually.

You know, I was recently told about one boy who came to the school only a short time ago, but has put in a lot of thought and also really learned something fundamental here with us. He said, "I don't know; I used to be in another school where we learned arithmetic and mathematics and geometry and all kinds of things; and now I'm supposed to become a good, capable person, but in this school I'm not learning any math at all. What am I going to amount to if I don't learn any math?" Where did this boy get the idea that he was not going to learn any math? You see, we try to accomplish under natural circumstances what other schools attempt to achieve by scheduling, by herding the children from one subject to another so that they never have time to concentrate on anything. So that the children can really work their way into a subject, we teach the same subject for weeks at a time during the main lesson of the day, for two hours each morning. We do not jump from one lesson to the next or from one subject to the next; we only change subjects after a while. Now this boy arrived at a time when mathematics was not being taught, so he thought that he was not going to learn any math at all. Later, of course, he noticed that he was then concentrating on math rather than being driven on to something different in each lesson; he was learning math more thoroughly. It is easy for misunderstandings of this sort to arise, even if they are not all as obvious as in this case. In the Waldorf School, many things look different from what we were used to earlier, so we should not be too quick to judge.

The things we foster really are drawn from what I have called "understanding the human being." This is characteristic of our school. It is also the reason why, as far as we can tell, the children are extraordinarily happy to come to school. I come to the school from time to time and take part in the lessons. We are striving to work out of the nature of the child in such a way that the children feel that they want to know the things we intend them to know, to be able to do the things we intend them to be able to do, rather than having the feeling that things are being forced upon them. This has to be developed in a way specific to each subject, since each one is different.

Next, all instruction must be pervaded by a specific educational principle that can be attained only if the teachers themselves are fully involved in spiritual activity. It is not possible for them to do this if they are not aware of their responsibility to the spiritual life. However, ladies and gentlemen, it is only possible to take up this great responsibility toward the spiritual life if it is not being replaced for us by a merely external feeling of responsibility. If we proceed simply according to what is prescribed for a single school year, we feel relieved of the need to research week by week both what we are to take up in school with regard to the individual subject, and how we are to present it. It should be characteristic of our teachers that they draw again and again from the living spiritual source. In doing so, they must feel responsible to the spiritual life and know that the spiritual life is free and independent. The school must be self-administrating; teachers cannot be civil servants. They must be fully their own masters, because they know a higher master than any outer circumstance, the spiritual life itself, to whom they stand in a direct connection that is not mediated by school officials, principals, inspectors, school boards, and so forth. The activity of teaching, if it is really independent, requires this direct connection to the sources of spiritual life.[2] Only teachers who possess this direct connection are then able to convey the spiritual source to the children in their classes. This is what we want to do; this is what we are striving to accomplish more and more. In the time since we began our work, we have carefully reviewed from month to month how our principles are working with the children. In the years to come, some things will be carried out in line with different or more complete points of view than in previous years. This is how we would like to govern this school—out of an activity

---

2. On truly independent educational activity and the threefolding of the social organism, see Rudolf Steiner's *Towards Social Renewal*, Rudolf Steiner Press, Bristol, England, 1992, [*Die Kernpunkte der sozialen Frage in den Lebensnotwendigkeiten der Gegenwart und Zukunft* (1920)], GA 23, 1976, and *The Renewal of the Social Organism*, Anthroposophic Press, Spring Valley, NY, 1985, in GA 24, *Aufsätze über die Dreigliederung des sozialen Organismus und zur Zeitlage* 1915–1921, 1961.

that is direct and unmediated, as indeed it must be if it flows from spiritual depths.

You absolutely do not need to be afraid that we are trying to make this school into one that represents a particular philosophy, or that we intend to drum any anthroposophical or other dogmas into the children. That is not what we have in mind. Anyone who says that we are trying to teach the children specifically anthroposophical convictions is not telling the truth. Rather, we are trying to develop an art of education on the basis of what anthroposophy means to us. The "how" of educating is what we are trying to gain from our spiritual understanding. We are not trying to drum our opinions into the children, but we believe that spiritual science differs from any other science in filling the entire person, in making people skillful in all areas, but especially in their dealings with other human beings. This "how" is what we are trying to look at, not the "what." The "what" is a result of social necessities; we must apply our full interest to deriving it from a reading of what people should know and be able to do if they are to take their place in our times as good, capable individuals. The "how," on the other hand, *how* to teach the children something, can only result from a thorough, profound and loving understanding of the human being. This is what is meant to work and to prevail in our Waldorf School.

This is what I wanted to tell you, my dear friends—to point out how on the one hand we need our children's parents to be really sincere friends of our school. The more we are able to know that this is the case, the better and more forcefully we will be able to accomplish our intentions for the school. We need to have an ongoing activity of love for teaching, of love for dealing with children, among our faculty and among all those who are connected to our teaching. This will be accomplished if a real spiritual life, a spiritual life that has honest and upright intentions with regard to humanity's spiritual, economic and political upswing and progress, stands behind our faculty and all those having to do with our school. It will be accomplished if the attitude toward teaching and the skill in teaching that are to be at work in our school are surrounded by a wall of parents who approach us with understanding and are devoted to our school in sincere friendship. If we have these friends, then the work of our school will succeed, and we can be convinced, ladies and gentlemen, that by doing what is good for our school and our children we will also be doing what is good for all of humanity as it is meant to evolve in the future. To work in the right way for education, for schooling, also means to work seriously and truly for human progress.

From the discussion

Herr Molt thanked Dr. Steiner for his lecture and encouraged the parents to ask questions and make their wishes known.

People complained that the children in the second grade could not yet read as well as those in the public school, and that because the subjects were being taught in blocks, the children always lost their connection to what had been done before.

Dr. Steiner replied:

With regard to reading and writing at the right time, I would still like to say the following: In line with what we are accustomed to today, it is certainly somewhat depressing to see a child going into the second grade who still cannot correctly rattle off what is there on the paper in the form of little ghosts. However, experience contradicts this and teaches us to know better. You see, we do not necessarily have to assess life only in terms of very short spans of time. I have met people who at the age of eighteen or nineteen were able to put their reading and writing to extremely good and skillful use, for instance because of being obliged to take up a career at an early age, as life sometimes demands of us. I have met people who found their place in a profession at an early age with considerable skill, and I have known others who did this with less skill. Now, do some research and find out whether, among these people whom life forced to embark on a career at age eighteen or nineteen, the ones who did so with skill are the ones who learned early, much too early, to rattle off what the little ghosts on the paper said, or whether it was the ones who learned to do this somewhat later. At issue here is whether things were learned in the right way for real life. This is what our method adheres to very carefully. I would like to make you aware that we often do not observe these things in their appropriate context in life. I have met people who had a very, very good style of writing, who wrote good letters. It was possible to research the circumstances to which they owed this. And I must confess quite openly that I discovered that in most cases they were people who had still made the most awful mistakes at age eight or nine. They only learned to shed these mistakes at age ten or eleven, but that is how they came by their special skill. These things are complicated, and we have to consider how our methods of instruction proceed from a comprehensive understanding of the human being. Then we will get used to the fact that many things become accessible to the children at different times from what we are used to. If it had always been the case that there had been strict rules about these things—"It is harmful for children to learn to read before the age of eight"— then no one today would be surprised when they still cannot read, but now we think this is a bad thing. There is something in this that you just said yourselves: The Waldorf School is supposed to lead to the right thing, not to make compromises with what is false.

As to what was said about it being difficult for the children to get back into a subject when they have been away from it for a while, what is important here is that we not judge the success of the school by what happens in the very next block of time. For the life of the mind, we need something similar to what happens in our physical life: We cannot be awake all the time; we must also sleep. When we do not sleep, we also cannot be properly awake in the long run. When the children have been taught for a couple of years according to this method, in which things do not always proceed at a constant pace but are removed from the children's view now and then, you will be able to convince yourselves how thoroughly they have taken possession of these things. After a couple of years you will probably come to a different conclusion than you do now on the basis of first impressions. Of course we are exposed to misunderstandings on some counts. However, perhaps what now puts people off will prove its worth over the years. We must wait and see.

Two additional questions addressed the points of whether Waldorf school students would be able to take the Abitur,[3] and of whether it would not be possible to assign homework.

Dr. Steiner responded:

It is certainly a matter of principle with us that the children should not be deprived of any possibility to take their place in life as we know it at present. There are certain things we have

---

3. The German school-leaving examination that qualifies a student for university entrance.

to do as a consequence of our pedagogical and methodological viewpoints, but these must be compatible with guiding the children into life in ways that do not cause them any outer difficulties. I formulated this principle myself, and it is being implemented as best we possibly can, especially in the most important points. With this in mind, I also drew up a document, an educational contract of a sort, that takes these two things into account.[4] We teach without regard for the interim educational goals that are set for the individual grades in other schools until our children are nine years old and have completed the third grade. After all, in order to do justice to what follows from a real recognition of the children's needs and to meet the demands of a real philosophy of education, we need a certain amount of leeway, don't we? After this amount of time, we can then take into account what is required of us by law for all kinds of underlying reasons. So, by age nine we want the children to have come far enough that they would be able to transfer to any other school. After that, we again allow ourselves some leeway until they are twelve, so that we can again practice an appropriate education during this time. At age twelve, any child is again able to transfer to another school. The same thing will apply at age fifteen and again at the *Abitur*. If we are lucky enough to be able to continue adding grades to the school and to take the children all the way to the *Abitur*, then they will be far enough along to take the exam at the usual age. Of course it is always possible that there will be an examiner somewhere who insists that the young people from the

---

4. When the Waldorf School was founded, Rudolf Steiner had submitted a memorandum to the authorities in which the agreement was recorded that at the conclusion of the third, sixth and eighth grades its students were to be at the same level of learning as their counterparts in the public schools. Within these time-periods, however, the School was guaranteed complete freedom of instruction.

Waldorf School cannot do a thing. It is always possible for the examiners to flunk someone if they so choose, or to give the slow ones a good grade and flunk the smart ones. We cannot guarantee that this will not happen. As a general rule, however, where we can do better than what is done outside, we must do better, in spite of the fact that we must avoid putting obstacles in the children's way when it comes to meeting the outer demands of life. To be sure, this is at best a second choice. It would be better if we could also establish colleges, but that cannot be, so we must be content with the second choice in this instance.

We should never fail to consider what it means for a real art of education when children are given assignments that we cannot make them complete. It is much, much better to refrain from giving compulsory homework, so that we can count on having the children do what they do with real pleasure and conviction, rather than constantly giving assignments which some children will not complete anyway. It is the worst thing in education to constantly give assignments that are not carried out. It demoralizes the children in a terrible way. We must be especially careful to comply with these more subtle educational principles. The children who want to work have plenty to do, but there should be no attempt at coercion on the part of the school. Instead, if we absolutely want the children to work at home, we should make the effort to encourage them to do so voluntarily. There will always be enough for them to do. But we should not let the tendency arise to work counter to the principles of a really appropriate art of education by moving toward coercion.

Address at the assembly at the end
of the second school year[5]

June 11, 1921

My dear children! I must speak to you first of all. You have now
put a year of school behind you. When you entered the classes
you are in now, you were one year younger, and now you have
grown one year older. This can remind you of how you are
always growing older, and this in turn will bring you to the
thought that someday you will have grown from being children
to being adults, big people who will have to be good and capable so that they can work and really carry out what the world
and other people ask of them.

Now recall how you were once very small. Remember how
you all used to be very little babies who could not speak. You
learned to speak and you learned many other things, and when
you had already learned a lot, you came here to us to go to
school. Your parents sent you here to go to school with us.
Think about your parents and about how they thought about
you. When you were babies, when you were very small children, your parents were concerned: "What will become of my
boy? What will become of my girl? Will they grow up to be
good and capable people someday, so that when I am old I will
be able to have confidence in my children?" That is what your
fathers and mothers said. And you know, dear children, that

---

5. When he was in Stuttgart, Rudolf Steiner always spoke at these final
assemblies, as he did at the opening assemblies. In the early years all the
teachers also addressed the children.

your parents brought you here, you who are nearest and dearest to them, so that you would grow up to be people like that. Your parents were concerned that you grow up to be good, capable people, and they brought you here to this Waldorf School because they believe that the teachers here can teach you to grow up to be good and capable people.

Remember that you must learn! Your parents brought you here and entrusted you to your dear teachers, and you must bring home a present to your parents at the end of each day and especially at the end of the year—a present that they will like a lot and that will make them say (if it is a good present), "My boy, or my girl, has learned something real." You must realize that it is something really nice for them when you can go home at the end of the school year and say, "Father and Mother, I really tried hard to learn something good." If you can do this, dear children, you give your parents great pleasure and take away one of their greatest worries. This is something we especially want to think about today. Let us think about being here in this school to fulfill what our parents intended when they brought us here.

After that, let us think about growing older each year, and about being grown-up people someday. Life is coming, with its pain, its destiny, and its joy, and with its work, too. Life, my dear children, will ask a lot of you. It will have very specific requirements for you. Now, dear children, there is one thing that always will give you strength, always be a sun for you, and that is being able to remember being here in school and gradually coming to love your teachers more and more. You do love your teachers very much, don't you? ["Yes!" answer the children.] Later, if you can think back to how you once learned something, to a nice day when your teacher spoke to you with love and it was a real joy for you to be in school, then you will really have a sun that shines into our life. Someday when you are really old and have gray hair, you can think back and remember learning something nice. And if you remember being in school in the right way, you will see that this gives you strength, and that something of it will last until the day you die.

There is something that makes remembering unpleasant, something that clouds our memory, and that is if we have to think, "Oh, I was such a lazy character!" It is not good later on in life if we have to think of how lazy we were. It has a very bad effect on our life if we have to remember that we did not love our teachers and that we had no love for the subject or for what was on the blackboard or for what was being said or read out loud. It is always lovely later on if we can remember working hard and loving the teacher, but it is painful when we have to say to ourselves, "I was a lazy kid. If I hadn't been so lazy, I would be a skillful person now." Maybe it was fun to be lazy, but later on you will regret it bitterly. Similarly, if you did not pay attention, you will understand nothing of life, and then your whole life will be like a sun with a big cloud in front of it that covers the whole world with hailstones. That is what it will be like if you have to remember not loving your teachers or not loving what you were taught. Keep this in mind, and your thoughts will be good when you think about working hard and paying attention and loving.

That is why you are here. You are here to grow up to be good, strong, capable people in life, and that can happen only if you can remember your childhood as a time when you tried hard to pay attention and to love your subjects and your teachers. That is what you should feel in every lesson. When you come to school in the morning and say your morning verse, you should remember that you are here to become a good and capable person. When you go home from school, you should be thinking about how every minute in which you are not hard-working, attentive and loving is a minute wasted because you are making your parents worry. You bring the best thing home to your parents if they say when they see you coming, "I can tell by looking at my children that they are bringing something good home from school today." Think about coming home to your parents after school. They should be able to say to themselves, "My children will grow up to be good, capable people." I want to tell you this, dear children, because we grow a little older each school year, and we remember how we are growing older.

Now that I have talked to the children, I would like to speak over their heads and say a few words to their parents. What unites this school's faculty is the recognition that a divine spiritual element pervades all human activity, and that people can devote themselves to this divine spiritual element. They must do so especially when they have tasks such as those that teachers have. Our teachers always must be aware that their task consists in calling the spirit of the world down into the school, and they must live in this awareness. This awareness, ladies and gentlemen, is best established among our faculty through the relationship we need to have to the parents of the school children. This relationship should be such that we really think together with the parents, that our feelings are in harmony with theirs, and that what we try to do in the school is the same as what the parents are trying to do with their dear children in realizing their ideals. Our teachers' philosophy hammers this into their hearts and souls every morning. By looking at the souls of the children, our teachers learn the value of the human soul and know the value of what you have given them by bringing your children here. You have given them the gift of being able to guide the spirit into human souls. It is with this deep feeling of gratitude and of good intentions that our teachers receive what is nearest and dearest to you, the children you bring to this schoolhouse. This is the source of our teachers' efforts to give something back to you, in love and gratitude and to the best of their abilities, in the souls you then see when your children come home from school or when they leave school to make their way in life. Our teachers receive a gift from you in the form of faith in human development; they would like to give a gift in return by educating your children to be good human beings. To be able to do this, they need to be in full agreement with you. You can be certain, ladies and gentlemen, that when you as parents strive toward this agreement and express it in the right way, harmoniously and with fellow-feeling, as you did just now, our teachers then feel that they have solid ground under their feet, regardless of whatever opposition and enmity they may encounter from other directions. May our teachers seek the impulse for their activity in this harmony with our parents.

There is still a third thing I would like to say to you, my dear teachers. You are united with the spirit of a spiritual world-view. With the best forces you have rooted in you, you try to understand the souls of growing human beings and to work on these souls, not in the sense of a school promoting a single philosophy, but in the sense of permeating an entire system of education with a thoroughly spiritualized attitude. This is the best way to learn two things, my dear friends.

The first is what wells up in freedom from creative strength, from within the human being. We gradually come to recognize that we must constantly learn what is good for the children from the children themselves. We learn to recognize that only what we create in freedom, the best in us that arises from our interactions with the children, can work into the children's souls. Our creative strength educates us, in the best sense of the word, to be able to do this, and we regard this as the best thing we can do in all of our work.

The other point is that because of our world-view we have developed a deeper connection to the idea of destiny. We work in an artistic manner on the souls of the children, but what we are working on is not like an outer work of art made of marble or wood; it is something that unites with us through destiny. When we stand in front of our children each day, trying to embody, ensoul, and enspirit them with the right insight that is present in the background, we unite with these souls for eternity as a matter of destiny. In the realm of eternity we will be met by what we have shaped during these different transformations, and by how we have done so. In a world-view such as the one we have, the teacher's true responsibility flows out of a feeling for freedom and destiny. It is out of the spirit of this responsibility that you, my friends, spoke earlier, both to the children and over their heads to their parents. I merely wanted to sum up your words.

Once again, let us say to you, children, "Come back to school next year with the same joy in paying attention; learn to love your teachers even more than you have until now; think of how your teachers' minds are focused day and night on having you grow up to be good, capable people. Your teachers show their love for you in their efforts to educate your souls, your spirits, and your bodies so that you will grow up to be good, capable people." Let us impress this deeply upon ourselves as we conclude this school year, and let us begin the next school year with the appropriate strength. Resolve to work hard and pay attention, to love your subjects and your teachers. Then things will go even better than they went this year.

Address and discussion at the first official members' meeting of the Independent Waldorf School Association[6]

June 17, 1921

Ladies and gentlemen! I call this first official meeting of members of the Independent Waldorf School Association to order. Before I go into the agenda, please allow me to welcome you most heartily in the name of the Board. Of course only a small number of the Association's members are here today; we welcome all the more heartily those of you who are able to be here. We have 1,400 members, and not nearly that many are here, but it is a pleasure to see that a considerable number have come.

To begin with, ladies and gentlemen, there are some things that need to be said with regard to the development of the Waldorf School up to this point. We now have two school years behind us. From various publications that have already appeared, you probably know that in this Waldorf School which Emil Molt founded, we aspired to something that could really bring about something new in various directions as a result of new pedagogical and methodological viewpoints and as a result of a universal humanitarian way of thinking. We aspired to release new forces that are needed in the field of education in order to counter the forces of decline that are so

---

6. This speech was revised by Rudolf Steiner himself for inclusion in the *Mitteilungsblatt für die Mitglieder des Vereins Freie Waldorfschule* [Newsletter for Members of the Independent Waldorf School Association], August 1921, Vol. 1. He did not, however, revise the discussion that followed.

apparent in our times. Understandably enough, something important must be done now in the realm of the educational system. Our task was not an easy one; in choosing the teachers, we needed to make sure that the spirit of a much-needed new pedagogical and methodological way of thinking, as we may call it, was alive and active in them.

In addition, the faculty first had to come to a common understanding of what our task would have to become as we got into the details of pedagogical and methodological activity. For this purpose, a pedagogical and methodological course was given prior to the opening of the school for the college of teachers as it was initially constituted. Instruction was then begun, attempting to take this course as a basis. In addition to this first somewhat longer pedagogical course, a shorter supplementary course was given before the start of the second school year, and a second supplementary course is taking place now before the third school year begins.[7] On the various occasions when I as the educational director was able to visit the school in the course of these two years, it became evident—and I say this after a conscientious investigation—that in spite of all the difficulties that some individual teachers had to overcome in themselves—difficulties due in part to outer circumstances and in part to the difficulty of the task itself—it has become possible for the spirit that prevails in our school to take hold of the college of teachers ever more strongly. We have been involved in an ascending development, and the way in which this spirit of the Waldorf School has settled down among us to

7. Supplementary courses: See Rudolf Steiner's *Meditativ erarbeitete Menschenkunde* (1947) (available also as the first four lectures, Stuttgart, Sept. 15, 16, 21, 22, 1920 in *Erziehung und Unterricht aus Menschenerkenntnis,* GA 302a), *Balance in Teaching* (Spring Valley, NY: Mercury Press, 1990) and *Menschenerkenntnis und Unterrichtsgestaltung* (Eight lectures, Stuttgart, 1921, GA 302), *Educating Adolescents* (Hudson, NY: Anthroposophic Presas, 1996).

an ever greater extent leads us to hope that we will also be able to note an ascending development in the Waldorf School spirit in the school year to come. It has become evident that the new teachers who joined the old ones as the expansion of the school made it necessary have found their way into the spirit of the Waldorf School with astounding rapidity. In this connection, we can say that this spirit of the Waldorf School is becoming something more and more alive, something you discover and are touched by as soon as you come into the school.

In this connection, after properly assessing the situation, we have only good things to note; we can hope that by developing the spirit we aspire to we will gradually get to the point at which we can offer clear evidence that the Waldorf School will be able to achieve its goal. This is what there is to report about the spirit that prevails in the school and in the teachers' conferences, about the spirit that was evident to me, as the one who had to verify it, in the attitude and way of thinking that prevails within the college of teachers. The college of teachers consists of its founder Herr Emil Molt and his wife in the role of patrons, so to speak, and of the people you know. By the very nature of the thing, the educational directorship has fallen to me, and I may say that in the teachers' conferences that have been held in my presence and in the classes in which I participated, which happened quite often in the course of these two years, what I have just described has certainly been evident.

This is all that needs to be noted in brief about this side of things; however, there is something that needs to be presented from the other side. This is something that I believed to be fully justified in saying in all kinds of talks before the opening of the school and at the opening itself, namely that the Waldorf School will only really fulfill its mission if other such schools are founded very soon. With a single school, of course, we can provide nothing more than a model and a pedagogical and methodological example. I believe I am justified in telling you this. Of course we will be able to produce a model and an example of this sort, but in our times this can only be a beginning. What is needed now is to carry the spirit of which we have spoken into the entire educational system in the sense of the threefold social organism. This threefolding requires a truly free cultural life with regard to education. The spirit of which we have spoken can be achieved only through the broadest possible dissemination of the idea of the Waldorf School. The Waldorf School must have successors, and this depends of course on interest in the school developing in the widest possible circles. It may be said that the active cooperation of the members of the Waldorf School Association, and also of the parents, demonstrates an admirable degree of interest. Unfortunately, however, the idea of the Waldorf School has not excited interest in wider circles; interest there remains extraordinarily low. Apart from the single small-scale and very gratifying attempt that has been made within Central Europe, the Waldorf School has not found any successors, and there are very few movements afoot to get such successors started.

We can also say that the interest has not been as great as expected from another point of view, namely that it takes money for even *one* model school to thrive. We have had to set things up in a way that involves adding one grade a year. When the school was founded, it had eight grades; last year we added the ninth grade, and with the beginning of the third school year, which takes place tomorrow, the tenth grade will be added. In this way, we will expand the school upward each year so that eventually our graduating students will be able take the *Abitur* and go straight on to various colleges and universities. There is still time for all this, but this is how we imagine the school's expansion to take place. Of course this requires constant additions to our physical space. In addition, our original idea, which was to found this school primarily for the children of associates of the Waldorf-Astoria factory, has broadened considerably. We have been getting more and more applications from all over the place; in this respect there is no lack of interest. Interest in increasing the size of the school, in expanding this one school, and in the spirit of the school is certainly already present. This is evident from the fact that we have students applying on all sides, and that most grade levels have several parallel classes.

The Board of Directors' report will mention the difficulties with regard to expanding the school.[8] We can see from all this that it is necessary to arouse interest in the school in a financial context. We really cannot say that the school has met with this interest in a financial sense. We encounter new financial worries each time an expansion becomes necessary. Already today the Board will present some of its concerns in its report to this official members' meeting. While on the one hand we can report considerable satisfaction with the school's spiritual progress, this must be balanced by reporting our concerns, which will increase greatly in the next few weeks. Naturally, the college of teachers cannot deal with these concerns; it already has a great deal to do in keeping up with the school's spiritual progress. This is something that must be taken to the broader public in the right way in the near future. We simply must awaken interest in financially supporting the Waldorf School, or else even the model that a single school provides will not be

---

8. Because of a ruling on the laws governing primary schools, the Waldorf School had to reapply for approval in the fall of 1920. This was granted under the proviso that starting in the 1922/23 school year it, like other private schools, was not to admit a new first grade and would have to decrease the number of students in the first four grades. However, as an experimental school the Waldorf School was expected to win an extension to this deadline. The ruling was later repealed.

able to develop in the appropriate way. It is to be hoped that if we succeed in raising the interest of the broader public in the spirit of the Waldorf School and its results, we will be able to meet our other need, namely to broaden the concept of the Waldorf School by founding other such schools as successors to this one. If this does not happen, establishing a model and an example is all that will be possible. This would certainly not do justice to the ideas and ideals of the Waldorf School movement.

This is what I wanted to present to you in my role as chairman of the Waldorf School Association.

From the discussion

E. Molt: I could not wish for a nicer task than to have to present Dr. Steiner with our heart-felt thanks for his loving leadership of the school. We know that we have him to thank for the successful growth of the school.

Dr. Steiner: Ladies and gentlemen! I would like to thank Herr Molt for his kind words, and all of you for agreeing with them. I believe I may also express these thanks in the name of the entire college of teachers of our Waldorf School. There can be no doubt that to the extent to which this college of teachers has been successful in building up the Waldorf School, this has only been possible because the entire college of teachers is deeply imbued with the need for the idea of the Waldorf School, because each individual member of this college of teachers is enthusiastically involved with the idea of the Waldorf School. From this enthusiasm comes the strength to work at something essentially new. We can rest assured that in spite of many difficulties, this enthusiasm will endure, and as a consequence the strength needed by those of us who must provide for the Waldorf School and its spiritual progress will also endure. And in this sense, since you may be able to believe that we in this school are working out of pure enthusiasm for the idea of the Waldorf School, you will also be able to accept the promise I would like to make, in my name and in the name of my dear friends in the college of teachers, to you who have taken such a deep interest in the Waldorf School. Please accept our promise that we will in future continue to work in the way that you have seen and in a way that will satisfy you.

Someone expresses the wish to have a chance to see the Waldorf School.

Dr. Steiner: I believe you would not get much out of seeing the Waldorf School itself, and that the faculty would not be able to conduct a tour tomorrow morning. If it is possible for you to modify your wish, perhaps you could take part in the opening assembly here in the *Stadtgartensaal* at 9:30 tomorrow, if there are not too many of you. Would it be possible for you to do this instead? I am sure the teachers will have no objections. And if you should wish to take a walk tomorrow evening after six o'clock, the members of the college will be glad to show you the building when school is not in session.

A member: Perhaps people can be allowed to visit the school on a certain day? The eurythmy lessons, for instance?

Dr. Steiner: Eurythmy belongs to our lessons, so the same objections would apply to it as to other classes. I would like to comment that the most that would be possible would be that we might decide to show visitors the empty school when the children and teachers are not there. There can be no question of visiting while school is in session. That is, such a visit could only take place after weighing it up carefully in consultation with those who hope to learn something by visiting the school—for instance, with people who want to see something of this school because they are trying to found a similar school elsewhere, because they themselves are doing something relevant to spread the idea of the Waldorf School. Seeing the school in operation would only come into question in infrequent cases of this sort. Of course we have already had many requests along these lines, but for purely pedagogical and methodological reasons it would not be possible to have it happen on a more general basis. Even a legitimate visit during a lesson is a cause of disturbance, a disturbance that is not justifiable in pedagogical terms. Anyone coming into the classroom disturbs the lesson. Sometimes there is a higher goal that justifies the disturbance, and we have to accept reasons of this sort. But we need to be sensitive to the fact that a lesson requires presence of mind and should therefore under no circumstances be subjected to visitation unless there is some urgent need.

I believe, therefore, that it is also the view of the other members of the college that the most we can allow is for you to see the classrooms, and even this would be burdensome at the moment. I can assure you that the classrooms will be well worth seeing once we are receiving a lot of financial support. But with regard to equipment that comes from endowments, people are probably much more likely to feel that they are getting their money's worth if they go and look at other schools. We, on the other hand, would only be subjecting ourselves to the danger of having them tell us that they didn't see anything, that the instructional materials are anything but ample, and that they want their money back!

With regard to eurythmy, let me remind you again that we have done everything possible to demonstrate what eurythmy is like. We have organized events where people could see what the Waldorf children do in eurythmy, and I hope that these events will continue. These are opportunities for you to convince yourselves of what the Waldorf children can accomplish in eurythmy. For pedagogical reasons, it does not seem possible to me for us to make exceptions in the case of eurythmy to what applies to the rest of the lessons.

So far we have accommodated to the greatest possible extent any legitimate wish people might have to inform themselves of what is going on in the Waldorf School, and people have taken advantage of the possibility to see the school to an equally great and not always desirable extent.

In this regard, nothing healthy can come of it if visitation and our interaction with the outer world are governed by any directives other than those the directorship and teachers' college of the Waldorf School see fit to issue. It does not seem possible to me for the school's leadership to receive any such directives from an Association. The issue here is that only a proper decision of the teachers' college can come into consideration in a matter like this, so it does not seem necessary to me to vote in the context of the Waldorf School Association on whether or not this should be permitted. How this matter is handled depends absolutely on the college of teachers. There has also been no motion to do otherwise.

. . . It does not work to have what I described in the first part, the spirit of the Waldorf School, on display for visitors. It has to be developed in the lessons, and this can be done only in the way in which it has been attempted so far. The only way in which the spirit of the Waldorf School can be presented to the public is through public testimonials of people who have children here, who are becoming familiar with our educational ideals; that is, through parents and others related to the school. There is no possibility of drawing attention to the spirit of the Waldorf School in any other way.

I can assure you that I know that this suggestion was made with good intentions, but in the past two years we have been accommodating on all sides. We must guard carefully against having people come who are merely curious. However, we will also continue to not turn away anyone who has legitimate grounds for getting to know the school.

Now that we have come to the end of our gathering, allow me to still express on behalf of the Board our hearty thanks to you for being willing to attend this first gathering. I hope the experiences you will be able to have will satisfy the interest you have demonstrated by being present here today. In this sense, I thank you in the name of the Board of the Waldorf School Association for being here today. Let me now call this first official members' meeting to a close.

Address at the assembly at the beginning of the third school year

June 18, 1921

Dear children! Today I will speak first to those of you who are here with us today for the first time and who will be getting together with your nice teachers over in the Waldorf School in the next few days.

My dear children! Until now, your time has been spent at home in your parents' house, and your good parents have taken care of you, taken care of you lovingly. You need only to do a little bit of thinking—you can already think enough to do that—to know how your parents began each morning by taking care of you. They made sure that your bodily needs were met, that you got the breakfast and lunch that you need so badly in order to live, and they also made sure that you could enjoy life, that you had a chance to enjoy flowers and plants and all the beautiful things there are in the world. Dear children, you can also already think about how glad your hearts were when your dear parents said something nice to you. Perhaps it did not always occur to you to be heartily thankful for what they do for you, but now that you are starting school, which is something very important for you, I would like to tell you this today: The more grateful you are for all the love your parents give you—and they are always trying to do more—and the more gratitude you show in receiving this love, the better children you are.

During all this time, your parents were realizing that their children would grow up to be big people, just like they are themselves. Once upon a time they had to realize that there was something they needed to learn in order to be able to provide for their children. They had to learn to work. And you see, if you want to work, you also have to think. They had to learn to think! And then your parents thought about where they would send their children to become good, capable people who would be able to handle their work and get on in life. Then the thought occurred to them to send you here to us in the Waldorf School, because they thought that you could learn something here about becoming good, capable people. I want you to think about how your parents sent you here so that you will be able to work someday. You cannot work without thinking. So that you will know that, I want you to promise to work in the **Waldorf** School.

In the Waldorf School we have made sure that you will be able to learn something, and we have also made sure that you will be able to find things you really like. From time to time you received something from your parents, a gift or a kind word, and then you said or thought or felt, "That's really nice!" And you see, if you really understand what is going on when you go to the Waldorf School in the next few days, you may also be able to say, "That's really nice! Going to the Waldorf School is a nice gift our parents have given us."

You will often feel that this is a nice gift. You see, we have to take care of the Waldorf School, and the teachers are people who care a lot. They made sure that the children will be able to say, "That's really nice!" It will be easy for you to say it's nice in the Waldorf School because we have made sure that the men and women who are going to be your teachers are really nice. You will meet good teachers who really like you. And actually, you will learn the most if you really love your teachers. This is what you have to watch out for, that you really, really love your teachers. If you do, then you will also learn well.

This is why I am telling you especially to notice the nice things your teachers will tell you. If you really love them, then you will do what they want, and then you will really learn a lot. I think you will often be able to say to yourselves, "How nice that our parents sent us to the Waldorf School!" And when you come into our school and sit in class, you will also always be able to feel that your teachers love you a whole lot.

You know that you are often tired in the evening. Often you were tired, and then you had to go to sleep, and in the morning you woke up again. While you are sleeping, you do not see anything or hear anything, but you are getting strong before morning comes. That is when other spiritual beings are awake. This is something you cannot understand yet. (That is why you have to go to school—to learn to understand things that you do not understand now.) Other spiritual beings are awake, and people must be able to give themselves up to these spiritual beings. They must learn to love and respect what they do not see. That is what the Waldorf School wants to give you, so that you will be good, thinking, hard-working children, and devout children, too. In the Waldorf School you are meant to become devout children, children who know that people also have something inside them that we cannot see. And as I said, even though you may not have understood very much of this now, that is why you are coming to the Waldorf School, where you will learn to understand it. This is something you must understand, or you will not get anywhere in life.

Now I am going to turn to your parents who have sent you here, and I am especially going to thank them for the confidence they show in the Waldorf School by sending us what is nearest and dearest to them. I would like to assure these parents that we who are trying to represent and implement the spirit of the Waldorf School are aware of the infinitely great responsibility we take on when you parents bring what is dearest to you here to become good and capable in life. Now that you have made the important and significant decision to send your children to the Waldorf School, we hope that your confidence in the school will be able to grow as you see Waldorf faculty striving to accomplish what you expect of us in educating your children in spirit, body, and soul. What has developed in the Waldorf School over the past two years gives us good reason to hope that what we do will merit your confidence. What we do, what our Waldorf faculty does, is what will confirm the confidence you now show in the school by entrusting to us what is dearest to you. Although what I have said may not be fully comprehensible to our dear children, they will find that they are able to pick it up again later.

Now that I have said this to our youngest children who are just beginning their school careers, I would like to turn to the older children who have already spent part of their time in school with us, and say a few words to them. And the first thing I would like to say to them is something I have come to love doing each time I come here, because it always gets a clear and unmistakable answer. Now that I have asked the youngest children to make sure that they start to love their teachers, I would like to ask you older children, who have been here before, whether you love your teachers. [The children answer, "Yes!"] You love your teachers because that is the way things should be. The way your teachers behave toward you will make you love them.

To the older children, I would like to say this: In your new grades, you will meet the same teachers that you had last year. You will continue with what you learned in the earlier grades. However, you should still think about what it means to move up a grade. Think about how moving up can remind us that in life we are always getting older and older. Especially today, when you are entering a new grade, you should look back a bit on the time when you were younger. You should think about all the things you now know because of what was taught to you in school, and now that you are moving up a grade you should think about needing to look into the future. The future, my dear children, is what we often try to hold in front of us in life. It is what you should hold in front of yourselves.

When you go out in the street, you see the older people around you. You see them leaving home to go to work and then coming home from work; you see them going out to do all kinds of things that need to be taken care of in life. When you go out in the street, you also see younger people who have just gotten out of school and who now have to apply what they learned in school for the first time. You see people who are older than you are and who have already learned something from life itself, who have experienced joy and sorrow in life. And if these older people speak to you, then they will tell you that they learned a lot about life through having learned real things in school. They will tell you that school prepared them to be working people and to be really human. If people take life seriously, you will almost always find that when they think back on their school days, they think, "What would I be now if I had not been nurtured by loving teachers during my school days, if I had not learned all the things that you can learn when you are young, the things that help you on in life and are a real support for you in life?" You find people walking around with gray hair, people on whom life has already left its mark, people who have matured. Most of them, when they reach the twilight of their life, think back on their own childhood whenever they see children. Now they think back to when they were sitting at their desks in school, and only now do they understand what they were able to take with them from that time. Only now do they really feel what it meant for their whole life.

Let me tell you today that if you love your teachers, if you work hard while you are sitting at your desks in school, then having been able to be in school in this way will be the greatest possible joy for you when you have grown old. The Waldorf School wants to make sure that you have something that will last you a lifetime when you think back on the school, when you apply what came to you in the Waldorf School to your life. The Waldorf School does not want to simply uplift you; it wants to let the difficulties of work, which do have to be there, alternate with joy and with what can bring you pleasure in life.

The Waldorf School wants to give this to all of you. You will see that you can take great pleasure in having done hard work, in having learned something difficult. You must not believe it when people say that school should turn everything into a pleasure. As a teacher, you cannot always arrange things so that the students learn everything as if they were playing a game. You will not find that we always turn learning into a game. There will also be times when it is hard for you, but when you see that your teachers are concerned that there also be a place for the hard things, you will be able to take pleasure in overcoming the difficulties. Then you will also be able to be glad that you are in the Waldorf School and that you can learn what you need to learn for life in this way. And those of you who have been here longer will have noticed that we are really trying with all our might to help you become people with a feeling for true human devotion, people who can look up to a spiritual, supersensible world. You will learn to understand the words "spirit" and "supersensible world" better and better as you move up from one grade to the next.

Today, then, try to think about growing older. Moving up through the grades in school shows you that people grow older. It reminds you that you need to be in school to make sure, both for your own sake and out of love for your teachers, that you pay attention and work good and hard so that you learn what you need to know for life.

Every hour of the day and night, your teachers are concerned about how to best introduce you to what you need for life. With strong will and with all the thoughts they can possibly have, they are looking for what you need. Of course this will be difficult for you, but they will make it as easy as possible. If they tried to teach it to you in the form of a game, you would not become good, capable people in life. Some things in life are difficult, but you will overcome them if you learn to overcome difficulties when you are still children.

You will go into the new school year in the right way. You will learn many new things, and some of what comes to you will bring you new joys. Some of it will show you the greatness and glory and breadth of the things in the world into which we human beings come. You will learn that what shines down from the moon and stars, what expresses itself and reveals itself in this world that speaks to us when the plants grow green and come up out of the earth in spring, what reveals itself in deep valleys and in the shapes of mountains and in minerals—that all this challenges us to lend a hand and bring forth the best that we can. It challenges us to learn to understand something about the world so that we can work in it. What is presented to you in your new grade will help you learn to better understand the greatness and glory of this world, of the divine deeds of lofty beings. You will learn that it is inherent in the nature of human beings to take their place in this divine world as workers who are able to do something because of what they have learned. The moment will come when you look out at the world and at the hard-working people who do so much, and if you yourself are not capable and have not learned anything worthwhile, you will be forced to ask yourself, "Now that I have grown old, what am I, since I made myself useless as a child?" This moment will come. As you grow old, think about how you can avoid this moment. You certainly can avoid it. The less you reject what your teachers ask of you out of love, the bigger and stronger you will be as you take your place in life. Think about this. Think about it each morning when you go to school. Think about that moment, and by being attentive in school you will become good, capable people who have no reason to reproach themselves in life.

My dear children, today in this serious moment there is something else I need to remind you. By now you will have seen how, once people have gotten gray hair and grown tired and old, they are carried out and their bodies are buried; the end of their life has come. That is only an outer ending. When this moment comes, a person's immortal soul rises up to the spirit of whom we all know. Just as you are now in a body, one day you will be spirit. Although people must prepare themselves for serious work in the world, they also must prepare themselves to enter the world in which they will live as spirit, just as we now live in bodies in this physical, sense-perceptible world. The body gets sick if it is damaged by the outer world or harmed by the weather, or the damage can come from inside. It is a hard destiny for some people when their bodies do not grow right, but it is a much worse destiny if people do not let their souls grow right. While you are in school, getting ready to do good and capable work, you are being guided so that you can also grow in your souls, in the spirit of humanity, so that you will become good and capable people not only in the eyes of other human beings and in the eyes of the world, but also in the eyes of God and the spiritual world. You will already have experienced this spirit in the Waldorf School. Remain in this spirit and become more and more conscious of it, the older you get.

As you advance from the beginning of the year to the end, your work and your worries increase. So think of a moment like this as something especially important, something that reminds you of how we human beings are standing in the midst of the divine world; of how you need to become strong and capable in body, soul and spirit; of how you think of your spirit, your soul and your body in your diligent striving for growth and health. This thought will help you. You will reach the point where it gives you strength each morning, so that you can prepare your deeds and your goals in the right way. Then you will be able to think about it with satisfaction in the evening. If you can say to yourselves, "I did my duty in school," you will be able to pass over into God's spiritual world when you sleep. Through what you experience in the Waldorf School, you must increasingly learn the meaning of the word "duty," and how duty plays into love for your work. This is something you must learn in the Waldorf School, and through all of this you will become good and capable people.

I am saying this to those who are already in the upper grades, who are entering a more mature age, who are already closer to the life in which they will have to work independently. You more mature children must think about how what I have just said applies to you. You who are now moving up into the higher grades are allowed to do so because of a special destiny that gives you the opportunity to know more than some others can. You have seen others who are already called upon to go to work out there in the world at a young age. They were your classmates; continue to love them. Think of them and consider them your friends. Thinking about them in the right way will make life move forward. Learn not only your subjects, not only what grows and thrives in you directly, but learn to love others too. Get to know each other and learn to really love your classmates. Learn that people are there for each other, that the Spirit Creator of the world endeavors most of all to work through the love that human beings bring toward each other. It is the worst thing for a school when the students do not love each other. Try to discover something lovable in each of your fellow students; there is something lovable in every human being. Learn to carry into each of your classes the warmth that expresses itself in love. If you learn to do that, what you have acquired in this way will give you much to carry out into life.

Now I would also like to address a few words to the parents whose children have been in the Waldorf School before. You will have done some thinking about our way of working in this school. Perhaps you have already been able to see that how we work here requires a sensitivity to the great needs of civilization at the present time. The people who brought the idea of the

Waldorf School into the world are burdened by the knowledge that things have come so far that we had to experience the great suffering of the beginning of the twentieth century, the great killing and the distress it brought with it. Those who observe all this with an unprejudiced view, ladies and gentlemen, know that attitudes and ways of thinking, things that live in human thoughts and human hearts, are the origin of these outer events. They know that we must work on the soul and spirit of humanity so that it can be guided out of the forces of world decline into forces of ascent. The idea of the Waldorf School was born out of the great thoughts of our times, and this responsibility stands over us as we work. We in the Waldorf School would like to imbue ourselves through and through with the idea of what it means to lay seeds in the hearts of children, seeds that must begin to grow in the next few decades for the salvation of the world.

At this point I always like to invoke the feeling of responsibility that lies in nurturing humanity's near future. Ladies and gentlemen, it is easy to speak of great ideals in an abstract sense. It is easy to proclaim that humanity must strive for the true, the beautiful and the good. But salvation and happiness in human evolution do not come from speaking great words about utopias and distant ideals for the future, or from nice words about things that are still undefined and unclear and hovering in the misty distance. They do not come from what we say to make ourselves feel good inside. Working for salvation and happiness and a livable society lies in grasping the details of the tasks life presents us with. If we can think about ideals and ideas in the right way, then ideas become something holy for all of us. If we talk about ideals as if they were undefined, nebulous things, we are speaking in hollow and empty words, but if we do not do that, if in all our dealing with ideals we are aware that we are involved in real concrete work on them, then we contribute much more to the progress and evolution of humanity than we do through beautiful-sounding talk.

The men and women who are Waldorf teachers really want to kindle their feeling of responsibility, really want to dwell in a right understanding of the world, in this attentive listening to what the world demands. May there grow from this spirit the forces that are needed to always do the right thing at any given moment. These forces only arise when we are able to look at the whole. We live our lives with no backbone, no spiritual backbone, if we are not in a position to think and work on behalf of real ideals in this way, if we speak in indeterminate words and foggy ideals. Therefore, I would like to say a few concrete words about the forces that are present in the hearts and souls of our teachers, the forces they will use to justify the confidence you parents place in them, the forces they will use to prove that it is no blind confidence that leads you to send your children to the Waldorf School and that our efforts to nurture the next generation for the sake of the salvation and happiness of humanity are based on understanding.

In thinking like this and in acting on this thought, we are fulfilling not only some pet idea or feeling, but a mission of our times. In acting in this way, we understand what we must do so that humanity can progress from this age of great misery to different age. We understand what can come of wanting to have our young people led with understanding. We know that sensitivity in guiding these young people will carry over into a near and difficult future.

It is in this spirit that I would like to turn to my dear friends the teachers. We have worked together, made an effort together, to bring this spirit into the Waldorf School. After careful self-examination, we can say today that in some respects we have succeeded in what we set out to do. We succeeded in developing this in a certain way so that our intentions of two years ago have become our practice of today. This will become ever more the case. As the faculty, carried by this spirit, finds its way to its tasks, the outer practice of Waldorf teaching, our outer way of acting, will be imbued more and more by this spirit. Through the fact that our faculty makes a daily effort to learn the art of bringing what is present in the Waldorf School spirit into outer life, this spirit will become ever more a reality, more fit for outer existence; it will grow and perhaps pull others along through its growing.

The important thing is for this Waldorf School spirit to be an example for people to follow. We can do but little in comparison to what humanity needs. However, it can work as a model if you make an effort to do more and more of what has met with understanding on the part of the parents. Then it will be possible to bring the Waldorf School spirit out of the Waldorf School and into the entire life of our civilization.

This is why I am thanking all of you in this moment when you, dear teachers, must set new tasks for yourselves. I thank you because I have been present to see how you have worked on yourselves and thus taken part in the progress of the good spirit here in the Waldorf School.

In this feeling of gratitude we will continue to work together, and we will attempt to understand each other more and more, so that the body of teachers becomes a unity. A school is only something whole when it is an organism out of which a unitary spirit-soul arises. This is what we promise the parents today, these are the intentions we undertake for the future, in the hope that they will become deeds in the same way that some of our earlier intentions have become deeds.

Now that I have turned to you with these words, I would like to sum it up in a few words that may perhaps be said here, in the context of the spirit of the Waldorf School. It would of course be presumptuous to speak these words if they were intended to characterize what has happened through the Waldorf School. However, they are of significance if we speak them, not as a command or as a point we want to hammer in, but as something we say to ourselves so that the forces can become even greater, as we tried to make it happen in the two previous years. Knowing that each individual field of activity expresses in miniature what is intended to happen in the world, we say to ourselves as children, parents, and teachers trying to unite and work together so that the Waldorf School may prosper, not presumptuously, but to our own hearts—"Onward, in the true spirit of the Waldorf School ideal!"

This is the call I wanted to utter to the spirits and souls of all of you, and especially from my heart to yours, today when we are leading our students into a new school year.

Address at the foundation-stone laying of the Waldorf School's new building[9]

December 16, 1921

To you, my dear friend Emil Molt, who first conceived the idea of this school, founded it, and have been involved with it ever since its founding; to you, dear Herr Weippert, who have placed your architectural skills in the service of this building; to

---

9. A night bombing in 1943 damaged this building extensively, filling in but not completely destroying the first floor, which served as the basis for the school's reconstruction in 1945. The foundation stone containing the verse was well protected under the main entry. The original building, which had been acquired and remodeled by Emil Molt, was not damaged.

you, my dear friends on the faculty, who decided at the very beginning to devote yourselves to working here in this school; to all of you from the Waldorf School Association and the Board of Directors of the *Kommenden Tag*[10] who have pledged your care, collaboration and guidance to this place which is dedicated to the salvation of humanity; to you members of the *Bund für Dreigliederung des sozialen Organismus* [Association for Social Threefolding] who have accepted the task of protecting the seed of a free spiritual life here in this school; and to you, my dear children, pupils of this school, who have been privileged to enjoy its first lessons and its education toward humanity, so to speak; to all of you I turn in this moment when, with hearts that are grateful to destiny, we gather to lay the foundation stone for this school building that has come about, through the concern of all involved, for our children and the student body. In laying this foundation stone, we send with it these words, which according to age-old custom are inscribed on the document that will be buried in it:

> May there prevail in young human beings
> what spirit power can furnish in love,
> May there work in them
> what spirit light can furnish in goodness,
> Out of certainty of heart
> and firmness of soul
> For the body's ability to work,
> For the soul's inwardness,
> For the spirit's brightness.
> To this end let this place be dedicated.
> May young sensibilities find here
> a human caring endowed with strength,

---

10. Magazine, *The Coming Day.*

devoted to light.
Those who place this stone
Are mindful in their hearts
Of the spirit that is to prevail here,
That this spirit may secure the foundation on which
liberating wisdom,
strengthening spirit power,
and the manifest spiritual life
Shall live, reign, and work.
To this there would bear witness
in Christ's name,
in pure intent,
and in good will:[11]

(signatures of Emil Molt, Herr Weippert, Rudolf Steiner, Marie Steiner, and members of the faculty, the Waldorf School Association, the Board of Directors of the *Kommenden Tag*, and Association for Social Threefolding.)

. . . . .

We place this document in the pentagonal dodecahedron, which is the symbol of the active power of the human heart and spirit, of the power that we will apply with all our strength to what is to come about in this school. Let us now place the pentagonal dodecahedron with this document into the ground.

---

11. No copy exists of the version of the verse that was sealed up in the foundation stone. It is reproduced here according to the stenographic record of what Rudolf Steiner read at the ceremony. An apparently earlier version, different in minor details, has been found in a notebook of Rudolf Steiner's. See *Wahrspruchworte—Richtspruchworte*, second edition, Dornach, 1953. [Translator's note: Neither version is included in Arvia MacKaye Ege's translation of selections from the *Wahrspruchworte*, (*Truth-Wrought-Words*).]

My dear friends, dear children, dear students of the Independent Waldorf School!

The Waldorf School was born out of the spirit of our times into a time of great trouble. A great misfortune broke in on humanity in the form of a terrible, catastrophic war, and after this catastrophe had subsided outwardly, it brought on times in which we had to consider how to begin to prepare a future for humanity in which forces of further evolution, of progress, of ascent out of great need and out of humanity's decline, could be nurtured. The school is among the things that can be most effective in carrying the forces of the present—which may in fact be able to do little good at present—over into a future in which they will be able to have a greater effect. And in these difficult times, when humanity had to turn to such thoughts of the future above all else, the idea came to our dear friend Emil Molt to take the initiative to let the Waldorf School come about. Today, on the day when this building that will expand the Waldorf School receives its foundation stone, let us recall this fruitful idea most heartily and most thankfully. At the time when our friend Emil Molt set about founding this school and conceived this idea, such an idea encompassed all the great issues of the present. There will come a time when it may be possible to see the founding of this school in a more objective light than is possible at the present moment with all the incredibly complicated and confusing circumstances that are still confounding humanity and preventing it from seeing in all clarity that such a place for young people, which proceeds from an independent cultural life, is above all else an absolute necessity for our times. That Emil Molt was able to conceive this idea out of his feeling for these great issues of our times will never be forgotten and will always be given due recognition wherever people have any understanding of such needs of humanity and of the great impulses of human evolution in general.

In order to inscribe it on your hearts, dear children, dear students, I must also recall the people who have decided to form this school's first faculty. You, dear children, who were the first to enjoy being taught in this school, should inscribe this on your hearts and souls: In the face of the immense great tasks that human beings have been given with regard to education for the sake of our human future and goals, becoming a teacher in this school was a great and significant decision. We must keep in mind, however, that for now the school has gained the confidence of people in the widest circles, we might even say throughout the world. If you look at what is happening, you know that there are human souls all over the world who not only know that there is a Waldorf school in Stuttgart, but are also actively interested in the question of what we are trying to accomplish with something like this. You, my dear children, should be mindful that you are the first to be taught in a school that is being looked at by people all over the world, and for good reason. Above all, you and all the rest of us should be aware with sincere gratitude that a momentous decision was needed to bring about this school's faculty, which is the first to subject itself to such world-wide scrutiny. But this body of teachers is also imbued with the idea and the impulses from which this school took its start. These teachers know that they are working, although within a limited context, for something that ultimately concerns human evolution as a whole. They have demonstrated their ability to apply their full strength, to continue to apply their full strength, for the sake of what must happen for this school as a result of this attitude and these impulses. We have already seen many flowers as this school unfolds. This will not be forgotten by those who have dedicated themselves to cultivating what is meant to be nurtured here in this school in an all-encompassing sense. And when, as I have often done, I ask you children who are to be educated here in this school if you love your teachers, and you answer in the affirmative, then the whole relationship between students and faculty tells me that you are in the process of allowing this spirit to gradually enter the school.

Now I am going to ask you once again, so that you can answer from your hearts, how it stands with your relationship to your teachers. Once again, dear students, dear boys and girls, I am going to ask you, "Do you love your teachers, and are you grateful for what they are doing?" If so, then say "Yes!" ["Yes!" shout all the children.]

Dear students, dear boys and girls, this is what you should always feel. If you do, then the right spirit will be present in the school. Only in the light of this spirit can we bring about what must happen here.

This school, whose foundation-stone laying we are celebrating today, must also consider a second thing. In a certain respect, the school stands here as an example of how children should be taught today. As a single school, however, it cannot be more than a model. People look at this model in the way I described before. When I was in Norway giving lectures a short time ago, I could see that even at this distance there were numerous people who were watching this school and intimately participating in it. What has been founded here is seen as a model school. What is still lacking, however, is the more widespread insight that founding a model school is not enough. It is not enough unless an insight into the necessity of founding such schools spreads throughout the whole world. It is not enough unless hundreds and hundreds of people join together in an international school association to found schools like this everywhere. Otherwise, the most that can happen will be that this small student body will carry out into the world what humanity needs to see fostered for the sake of its evolution.[12]

However, we have not yet been able to find this second thing out there in the world. My dear friends, if we were in a position to found schools modeled on the Waldorf School in many places, if we were to receive the means to do so out of a clear blue sky, these schools would be filled all over the world. Not one of these schools, paid for with money from out of the blue, would stand empty. But what is lacking in the world today is the sense for social sacrifice. The impulse is strong enough to want to found schools like this everywhere, but it does not manage to move from outwardly acknowledging an idea that is necessary for our times in the strongest sense of the word, to actually summoning the will to accomplish what these times require. And the idea of the Waldorf School will not accomplish its task until this impulse is fulfilled in the world.

To accomplish this task requires many people who approach it with understanding. If it were possible for us today—we can only do it through thoughts—to establish inwardly as well as outwardly through this deep inner foundation we are laying in burying the foundation stone for this school building, to lay a foundation stone in the hearts of many people as a seed of what we hold necessary for humanity's evolution and ultimate goal, then a lot would have been done.

---

12. In the summer of 1920 Rudolf Steiner assumed that the founding of an International School Association was imminent. This Association was to awaken a feeling for independent spiritual life in the broadest possible circles and to create as quickly as possible the means for establishing schools independent of the state, wherever this was still possible under national laws. When people later set out to make the Association a reality, Rudolf Steiner said that the time in which an independent spiritual life could have been initiated was over.

Dear boys and girls of the Waldorf School, I speak to you all out of a heart and soul that are inwardly moved, so that in this solemn moment we can direct the forces in our hearts to what has just been described as necessary for humanity, to what has been indicated in the idea of the Waldorf School. When what is meant to live in human hearts actually is alive in them, they do possess a certain strength.

My dear friends, dear children, dear boys and girls of the Waldorf School! When people in ancient times prepared to lay the foundation for a building, they buried something living in the earth along with the document which stated the goal and purpose of the building and the names of those involved in its construction. This idea became more and more spiritualized. Today we exercise our sacred freedom in burying in the earth a symbol of the spirit, the pentagon dodecahedron that contains our promise, given in the name of Christ out of our pure intentions and our active working strength—however we may apply it. Today we place this symbol in the earth like a seed, having directed toward it the most beautiful thoughts of which we are capable.

And just as the forces of the world bring forth a living tree from a seed buried in the earth, let there come forth from what we have buried in the earth—steeped in our heartfelt wishes that the reason for this building's construction may flourish, steeped in our inmost hopes and expectations for the future— let the flower of what we have buried in the earth, of the thoughts and feelings and impulses of will whose symbol is our foundation stone, be what we must again and again call the goal and impulse of the Waldorf School—that it may be a place in which to nurture everything humanity needs for new moments in its progress, its civilization and its culture. May this flower spring up from the spiritually living seed that we are burying in the earth today.

You, dear children, dear boys and girls of the Waldorf School, are to be the first to unite your feeling and good will and good intentions with what has been said to you on this festive occasion. It is the true foundation stone of the Waldorf School, of what is meant to grow and bloom here on this site and to evolve on behalf of the well-being and goal of humanity.

1 9 2 2

Address and discussion at a parents' evening

May 9, 1922

Ladies and gentlemen! What I would like to do on this occasion is not actually to give a lecture, but rather to encourage as widespread an understanding as possible between those who are involved in the leadership and work of the Waldorf School and the parent body. The reason for this is that I really believe that this understanding, this working together of the parents with the teachers and others involved in the leadership of the school is something extraordinarily necessary and significant.

Allow me to begin by describing an experience I had not long ago, an experience that will illustrate the importance of the issue I have just pointed out. Several weeks ago it was my task to take part in the festival in Stratford-on-Avon in England, a festival organized to celebrate the birthday of Shakespeare.[1] This Shakespeare festival was one that took place wholly under the influence of education issues. It was organized by people who are deeply interested in the education of children and adults. It can also be said that during this entire festival the world of

---

1. Rudolf Steiner was invited to address the conference of the "Organization for New Ideals in Education" in Stratford-on-Avon, England, April 1922. He spoke on "Drama and its Relationship to Education" and "Shakespeare and the New Ideals." Included in *Waldorf Education and Anthroposophy 1*, Anthroposophic Press, Hudson, NY, 1995 [*Erziehungs- und Unterrichtsmethoden auf anthroposophischer Grundlage*, GA 304, Dornach, 1979.]

Shakespearean art merely provided a background, since the actual issues that were being dealt with were contemporary issues in education. On this occasion one of the small effects, or perhaps even one of the large effects, of the pedagogical course that I held at Christmas at our Goetheanum in Dornach became evident.[2] Some of the people involved in this Shakespeare festival had taken part in this course.

Now, not far from London there is a boarding school which is not very large yet, but which is headed by a person who was present at the Dornach course and who took from there the impulse to introduce what we can now call Waldorf pedagogy, the Waldorf system of education, into this boarding school and perhaps also to apply it in expanding the school.[3] We were invited to see this educational establishment, and in the course of the visit various questions were raised regarding how the school is being run at present and what could be done to transplant the spirit of the system of education that is fostered here in the Waldorf School to their situation.

One question in particular came up for discussion. The people in charge said that they were doing well with the children; each year they accept as many children as the small size of the establishment permits. The most difficult thing for them, however, was working together with the parents, and the reason for the difficulty—and this is certainly an international concern—was that nowadays the older generation everywhere has certain very specific views on how education is supposed to proceed. There are many reasons why parents send their children to one boarding school rather than another. But when there actually is

---

2. *Soul Economy and Waldorf Education*, Anthroposophic Press, Hudson, NY, 1986 [*Die gesunde Entwickelung des Menschenwesens*],16 lectures given in Dornach, 1921–22, GA 303, Dornach, 1978.
3. Known at that time as the Priory School, this is now the New School in Kings Langley.

a slight deviation from what they are accustomed to, it is very easy for disagreements to arise between the school and the parents. And this is something that really cannot be tolerated in an independent system of education.

The boarding school in question was experiencing especially great difficulties in this regard. What I am attempting to do now is neither to criticize nor to make recommendations, but simply to state the facts. In this school, in spite of the fact that it is a residential facility, there are no domestic employees at all. All the work of maintaining the school is done by the children and teachers. Cleaning the hallways, washing the dishes, planting the vegetables, taking care of the chickens so that they provide eggs—the list could go on and on. The children are involved in all kinds of work, and you certainly get the impression that things are run very differently there than in most other boarding schools. The children also have to cook and do everything else, and this goes on from first thing in the morning until late in the evening. It is also evident that the teachers and residential staff put a lot of energy into doing these things with the children. As I said, my intention is neither to criticize nor to advocate what they are doing; I only want to present it to you. Now it can happen that when the children go home on vacation and tell their parents about everything they have to do, the parents realize that they had not imagined it like that, and they cannot understand it. That is why it is so difficult to sustain harmony with the parents in this case. I describe this case only in order to point out how necessary we feel it to be, if we take a system of education seriously, to work together in complete harmony with the children's parents.

Now of course our situation in the Waldorf School is different. We have no residential facility, we simply have a school where we naturally have to keep the principles of child-rearing in mind while providing academic instruction. Nevertheless, you can rest assured that working together with the parent body is a fundamental element in what we in the Waldorf School regard as our task. In running the school, an infinite number of questions constantly arise with regard to the weal and woe of the children, their progress, their physical and mental health—questions that can be solved only in partnership with the parents. This is why it will actually become more and more necessary for these parents' evenings to evolve—and all the circumstances will have to be taken into account—and to become a more frequent event in the running of our school.

Our Waldorf School is meant to be a truly independent school, not only in name but in its very essence, and simply because it is meant to be an independent school of this sort, we are dependent on help from the parent body to an extraordinary extent. It is my conviction that if we have the desire to work together with the parents, this will call forth nothing but the deepest satisfaction on the part of all the parents.

The Waldorf School is an independent school. You see, ladies and gentlemen, what it actually means to be an independent school must be stated over and over again, and it cannot be stated strongly enough for the simple reason that in broader circles today it is scarcely possible to realize the extent of our need for independent schools of this sort. The prejudice of thousands of years is working against us, and this is how it works.

We do not need to look back very far in humanity's evolution to find a school system, especially a primary school system, that was independent to a very great extent. But at that time independence caused a lot of illiteracy because few people sought out formal education. Then, in the course of humanity's evolution in civilized areas, the desire began to grow in people to promote a certain educational basis for our interactions in society. At this point I cannot go into how this desire arose, but it came about at a time when people had renounced their allegiance to the old gods and now expected to receive all the blessings of humanity's evolution and everything needed to advance it from a new god, the god of the State. Central Europe in particular was an area where people were especially intent on seeing the god of the State as a universal remedy, especially in the education of children.

In those times, the principle that was applied as a matter of course was that parliaments and large advisory bodies and so on were gatherings in which geniality could flourish, even if the individuals involved in these representative gatherings were not impressive in their degree of enlightenment. The opinion prevailed that by gathering together, people would become smart and would then be able to determine the right thing to do in all circumstances.

However, some individuals with a very good and profound understanding of these matters, such as the poet Rosegger,[4] for example, were of a different opinion. Rosegger coined the expression—forgive me for mentioning it—"One person is a human being; several are people; many are beasts." Although this puts it a bit radically, it does contradict the opinion that has developed in the last few centuries, namely that all things state-related will enable us to determine what is right with regard to educating children. And so our school system simply continued to develop in the belief that there was no alternative to having everything spelled out for the school system by the political community.

Now, an independent school is one that makes it possible for the teachers to introduce into the educational system what they consider essential on the immediate basis of their knowledge of

---

4. Peter Rosegger, 1843–1918, Austrian teller of folk tales.

the human being and of the world and of their love for children. A non-independent school is one in which the teacher has to ask, "What is prescribed for the first grade? What is prescribed for the second grade? How must the lesson be organized according to law?"

A free school is one in which the teachers' actions are underlain by a very specific knowledge of how children grow up, of which forces of body and soul are present in them and of which ones must be developed. It is a school in which the teachers can organize what they have to do each day and in each lesson on the basis of this knowledge and of their love for children. People do not have a very strong feeling for how fundamentally different a non-independent school is from an independent school. The real educational abilities of the teachers can develop only in an independent school.

That people actually do not have any real feeling for these things at present is the reason why it is so difficult to continue to make progress with an independent school system. We must not succumb to any illusions in this regard. Just a few hours before leaving to come here, I received a letter informing me that after a long time had been spent working to open a school similar to the Waldorf School in another German city, the request for permission had been turned down. This is a clear sign that the further evolution of our times will not favor an independent school system. This is something I want to ask the parents of our dear schoolchildren to take to heart especially: We must lavish care and attention on this Waldorf School we have fought for, this school in which the independent strength of the faculty will really make the children grow up to be all-around capable and healthy human beings. We must be aware that, given the contemporary prejudices we confront, it will not be easy to get something like a second Waldorf School. At the same time, it should be pointed out that this Waldorf

School, which has not yet been in existence for three years, is something that is presently being talked about all over the civilized world. You see that it is nonetheless of significance— think about what I said about the school near London—that a group of people have gotten together to bring a Waldorf School into existence there.

We can also look at this issue from the much broader perspective of the need to do something to restore the position of the essential German character in the world. You can be sure, however, that the significance of this German essence will be recognized only when its spiritual content, above all else, is given its due in the world. This is what people will ask for if they meet the world in the right way. They will become aware of needing it.

For this to happen, we really need to penetrate fully into the depths of this German essence and to become creative on the basis of it. This is evident from something such as the vehement, sometimes tumultuous educational movement that could be experienced at the Shakespeare festival, which showed that there is a need all over the world for new impulses to be made available to the educational system. The impossibility of continuing with the old forms is a concern for all of civilized humanity.

The fact of the matter is, the things that are being fostered in the Waldorf School give us something to say about educational issues that are being brought up all over the world. But we also have almost all of the world's prejudices against us, and we are increasingly faced with the prospect of having our independence taken away, at least with regard to the lower primary school classes. It is extraordinarily difficult to combat these prejudices, and the Waldorf School can do so only by making its children grow up to be what they can beonly as a result of the independent strength of the faculty.

For this, however, we need an intimate and harmonious collaboration with the parent body. At an earlier parents' meeting I was able to attend, I pointed out that simply because we are striving for an independent school system, we are dependent on being met with understanding, profound understanding, on the part of the parents. If we have this understanding, we will be able to work properly, and perhaps we will also be able after all to show the true value of what is intended with the Waldorf School.

At that time I emphasized that we must strive to really derive our educational content from an understanding of the being of the child and the child's bodily nature. Since to observe the child is to observe the human being, it is possible to observe children in this way only if we are striving for an understanding of the human being as a whole, as anthroposophy does. We must say again and again that it is not our intention to introduce anthroposophy into the school. The parents will have no grounds for complaining that we are trying to introduce anthroposophy as a world-view. But although we are avoiding introducing anthroposophy into the school as a world-view, we are striving to apply the pedagogical skill that can come only from anthroposophical training as to how we handle the lessons and treat the children. We have placed the Catholic children at the disposal of the Catholic priest and the Protestant children at the disposal of the Protestant pastor. We have independent religious instruction only for those whose parents are looking for that, and it too is completely voluntary; it is set up only for those children who would otherwise probably not take part in any religious instruction at all. So you see this is not something we stress heavily. Whatever we have to say with respect to our world-view is strictly for adults.

But I would like to say that what anthroposophy can make of people, right down to the skill in their fingertips, applies especially to teachers and educators. In dealing with children and with instructional content, what we should strive for is to have the children find their way quite naturally into everything that is presented to them in school, as a matter of course. We should assess carefully in each instance what is right at a particular stage of childhood.

You know that we do not introduce learning to read and write in the same way that is often used today. When the children begin to learn to write, we develop the shapes of the letters, which are otherwise something foreign to them, out of something the children turn to with inner contentment as a result of some form of artistic activity, of their artistic sense of form. The reason why our children learn to write and read somewhat later is that if we take the nature of the child into account, reading must come after writing.

Those who are accustomed to the old ways of looking at things will object to this, saying that the children here learn to read and write much later than in other schools. But why do children in other schools learn to read and write earlier? Because people do not know what age is good for learning to read and write. We should first ask ourselves whether it is altogether justified to require children to read and write with any degree of fluency by the age of eight.

If we expand on these ways of looking at things, more comprehensive views develop, as we can experience in a strange way: Anyone who knows a lot about Goethe knows that if we had approached him with what is demanded academically of twelve-year-olds today, he would not have been able to do it at that age. He would not have been able to do it even at age sixteen, and yet he still grew up to be the Goethe we know of.

Austria had an important poet, Robert Hamerling.[5] As a young man, he did not set out to become a poet—that was

5. Robert Hamerling, 1830–1889.

something his genius did for him. He wanted to be a high school teacher, and he took the teacher certification exam. It is written in his certificate that he demonstrated an extremely good knowledge of Latin and Greek, but that he was not capable of handling the German language well and was thus only fit to teach the lowest class. But he went on to become the most important modern poet of Austria. And he wrote in the German language, not in Slovakian.

Our educational impulses must take their standard from actual life. The essential thing about our method of education is that we keep the child's whole life in mind; we know that if we present the child with something at age seven or eight, this must be done in such a way that it will grow with the child, so that it will still stay with the person in question at age thirty or forty, and even for the rest of his or her life. You see, the fact of the matter is that the children who can read and write perfectly at age eight are stunted with regard to certain inner emotional impulses that lead to health. They really are stunted. It is a great good fortune for a child to not yet be able to read and write as well at age eight as is expected today. It is a blessing for that child's bodily and emotional health.

What we need to foster must be derived from the needs of human nature. We must have a subtle understanding of this, and not merely know the right answer. It is easy to stand in front of a class of children and to figure out that this one said something right, but that one said something wrong, and then to correct the wrong thing and make it right. However, there is no real educational activity being practiced in that. There is nothing essential to the human development of a child in having the child do compositions and assignments and then correcting them so the child is convinced that he or she has made mistakes. What is essential is to develop a fine sense for the mistakes the children make. Children make mistakes in hundreds of different ways. Each child makes different mistakes, and if we have a fine sense of how different the children are with regard to the mistakes they make, then we will discover what to do to help them make progress.

Isn't it true that our perspectives on life are all different? A doctor does not have the same perspectives on an illness that a patient has. We cannot ask a patient to fall in love with a particular illness, and yet we can say that a doctor is a good doctor if he or she loves the illness. In our case, it is a question of falling in love, in a certain respect, with the interesting mistakes the children make. We get to know human nature through these mistakes. Excuse me for expressing myself radically, but these radical statements are really necessary. For a teacher, keeping track of mistakes is more interesting than keeping track of what the children do right. Teachers learn a lot from the children's mistakes.

But what do we need in addition to all this? We also need a strong and active inner love for human beings, for children. This is indispensable for teachers. At this point innumerable questions arise. We are concerned about a particular child's health of body and soul. We see this child for a few hours a day; for the rest of the time we must have confidence, complete confidence, in the child's parents. This is why the teachers and educators of our Waldorf School always appeal to this confidence, and why they are so eager to work in harmony with the parents for the well-being of the children. As a rule, this is not something that is aspired to in a non-independent school to anywhere near the same extent; there people stick to observing the rules. That is why the very idea of independence in education often meets with very little understanding today.

In some countries, if you talk about independent schools, people will tell you that while things may be like that in Germany, they do not need to found independent schools because their teachers are already free. Teachers themselves will tell you that. It is astonishing that they respond like that, because we can tell that the people who are answering no longer have any idea that they could feel unfree. They do what they are ordered to do. It does not occur to them that it could happen differently, so they do not even feel that things could be different.

Just think of how different your situation is from other people's with regard to understanding the Waldorf system of education. Other people have to make an effort to understand when we tell them we want to do things in a certain way because we believe it is the only right way. I believe that as parents of Waldorf School children you can see directly, in the beings that are dear to you, what is being done in the Waldorf School and how the relationship of the entire school to the child is conceived. It would be nice if there would come a time when it would be enough for parents simply to be content with what is being accomplished in an independent system of education. Today, however, all of you, who can see results in your own flesh and blood of how this Waldorf School is trying to work, must become strong and active defenders and promoters of the Waldorf system of education.

We have many other difficulties in addition to this. You see, if we really could live up to our ideals, we would be able to say that according to our insight, we should do this particular thing when the children are six, seven and eight, and this other thing when they are nine, ten, eleven and twelve, and so on. The results would be the best if we were able to do that, but we cannot; in some respects we must accept a compromise, because we cannot deny these children, these human beings who are growing up, the possibility to take their place in life.

So we have decided to educate the children from the time when they first enter primary school up to age nine in a way that is free of outer constraints, but while we are doing what human nature requires, at the same time we will support the children in a way that will enable them to transfer to another school [at the end of that time]. The same applies to age twelve and to age fourteen or fifteen. And if we have the good fortune to be able to continue adding grades, we must also make it possible for the young ladies and gentlemen who complete these grades to enter universities and technical colleges. We must make sure that the children will be able to enter these institutions of higher learning. I think it will be a long time before we are given the possibility of granting graduate or undergraduate degrees. We would accomplish much more if we were able to do that, but for the time being all we can do is to enable first the children and then the young men and women to learn what is required in public life in a way that does not inflict great damage upon them.

We find ourselves in very serious difficulties in this regard. You see, if you assess the situation according to human nature, according to what is good for human beings, then you would say that it is simply terrible for young men and women to be in modern college-preparatory and vocational high schools at the age of fourteen, fifteen, sixteen, seventeen. It estranges them from all of life. We must do what is necessary, whatever we can do, to make sure at least that the body also achieves a degree of skill that makes it fit for life. I often mention that you meet grown men nowadays who are incapable of sewing on a button for themselves if one gets torn off. I say this only by way of example. There are other similar things that people also cannot do, and above all they do not understand anything about the world. Individuals need to stand there in the world with their eyes open so that their hands are free to do whatever is needed. You see, this is why at a certain age we need to introduce the elementary aspects of things like spinning and weaving. Now, however, when students graduate from ordinary schools, they are not tested in weaving and spinning or in other arts that are useful in life, and so we must do these things in addition to all kinds of things that are required for the exam. This means that we must arrange our lessons as economically as possible. There is a special art to this in teaching.

Perhaps I may be permitted to introduce an example that happened to me personally. It was a long time ago. A family had entrusted their children to me for tutoring, and among them was an eleven-year-old boy who had been given up on as far as education was concerned. He was eleven years old, and for my information they showed me a sketchbook in which he had demonstrated his drawing ability. This sketchbook had a gigantic hole in the middle of the first page. He had done nothing but erase; that was all he could do. He had also once taken the test for entry into the first grade, and could do nothing at all. With regard to his other behavior, he often did not eat at the table but went into the kitchen and ate the potato peels, and there were difficulties in many other respects as well. It was a question of accomplishing as much as possible in the shortest possible time. I often had to work for three hours to get the materials together for what I would present to the boy in fifteen minutes. After two years he had progressed to the point where he could enter the *Gymnasium*. He was a hydrocephalic, with a huge head that steadily became smaller.

I mention this case because it shows what I mean by economy of instruction. Economy of instruction means never spending more time on something with the children than is necessary according to the requirements of physical and mental health. Nowadays it is especially important to practice this economy of instruction because life demands so much. Our Latin and Greek teachers, for example, are in a difficult situation because we have much less time to spend on these things, and yet they still have to be fostered in a way that meets the legitimate demands of cultural life. In all subjects, we must seek the art of never overburdening the children. And I must say that in all these things, we need to be met with understanding on the part of the parents; we need to work together in harmony with the parent body.

Really, the genuine successes that are of the greatest significance for life do not lie in accomplishing something amazing on behalf of one or the other gifted student. Genuine successes lie in strength for life. Thus it is always deeply satisfying to me when it happens that someone says that a certain child should be moved from one class to another so that this or that can be accomplished. The teacher fights for each and every child from time to time. These are real successes that take place within the loving interaction between the faculty and the children. Something can come of this, and things on which such great value is placed, such as whether the children are a little ahead or a little behind, fade into the background in comparison.

We are already being confronted with the fact—again, I would like to put it radically—that we cannot possibly be praised by those who hold the usual opinions about today's school system, who are coming from these opinions. There is always something wrong in believing that something would be accomplished if people who think like this were to praise us. If that was how things were, if we were praised by today's school authorities or by people who believe that these authorities are doing the right thing, then we would not have needed to start the Waldorf School at all.

Thus it is a matter of course for us to depend on the parents being in harmony with us and giving their time and attention to a method of education that derives from what is purely human. This is what we need today, and in a social sense, too.

Social issues are not resolved in the way we often imagine today. They are resolved by putting the right people into public life, and this will happen only if people are able to grow up really healthy in body and soul. We can do very little to influence what is specific to an individual, what an individual is capable of learning on the basis of his or her particular abilities, because in order to be of service at all in educating a person to become the best he or she can be—if we had to teach a Goethe, for example—we as teachers would have to be at least the equal of the person we are teaching. We can do nothing about what an individual becomes through his or her own nature; there are other factors determining that. What we can do is to remove obstacles so that individuals find the strength within themselves to live up to their potentials. This is what we can do if we become real educators and if we are supported by our contemporaries.

First and foremost, we can be supported by the parent body. We have found an understanding body of parents. Certainly, what I have to say tonight is filled with a feeling of gratitude. That so many of you have appeared tonight gives me great satisfaction. I hope we will be able to talk about details in the discussion period to follow; our teachers are prepared to answer any questions you may ask. Before that, however, I would still like to point out certain characteristic traits.

Recently the Waldorf faculty and I held a college-level course in Holland.[6] The afternoon session in which pedagogical issues were discussed was led by Fräulein von Heydebrandt of the Waldorf School.[7] This was one of the most interesting afternoons because we saw that today's educational questions are of concern all over the world. Of course we know that we have no right to harp on how wonderful it is that we have come so far; we are not trying to emphasize our accomplishments.

---

6. Six lectures in The Hague, April 7–12, 1922. See *Die Bedeutung der Anthroposophie im Geistesleben der Gegenwart*, Dornach 1957.
7. Caroline von Heydebrandt, 1886–1938.

The way things are today, many people recognize the impulse behind our school. What is still lacking, however, is for them to stand energetically behind us so that this cause can win additional support and become more widespread. Of course we realize that the first concern of parents is to have the best for their children. But with things as they are today, the parents should also help us. Going through with this is difficult for us. We need help in every respect; we need the support of an ever growing circle so that we can overcome the prejudice against our method of education. I say the following with a certain reserve; I certainly want to remain convinced that those who are sitting here have done everything they can financially. I am speaking under this assumption so that none of you will think that I want to step on your toes. Nonetheless, the fact remains that if we want to go forward, we need money.

Yes, we need money! Now people are saying, "Where is the idealism in that? What are you anthroposophists doing, telling us you need money and pretending to be idealists?"

Ladies and gentlemen! Idealism does not stand on firm ground if it makes grandiose statements but says, "I am an idealist, and since I am an idealist, I despise my wallet. I do not want to get my fingers dirty; I am much too great an idealist for that!"

It will scarcely be possible to make ideals into reality if people are such great idealists that they are unwilling to get their fingers dirty when it comes to making financial sacrifices. We must also learn to strike the right note in public in suggesting to people that they give us some support in this matter, which is still a great and terrible cause of concern for us.

After all, the Waldorf School is big for a single school; it has enough students. It is almost not possible to maintain an overview any more. This is a concern that has to be taken very seriously. We certainly do not want the school to grow larger in its present circumstances; we are going to give in to the need for physical expansion. But then the number of students will increase, as will the number of teachers. And since teachers cannot live on air, this requires the means to support them.

I am assuming, ladies and gentlemen, that each of you has already done whatever you can. It is now a question of spreading the idea further in order to find the idealists out there. There must be a decision on the part of the parent body to help the Waldorf School with regard to its material basis, or I am afraid that in the near future, if we want to continue to take care of things properly, our worries will become so great that they prevent us from sleeping, and I am not sure that the teachers in the school will be the kind you want to have there if they are no longer able to sleep at night!

Some people may have the feeling that I have been too radical in my choice of some of the things I have pointed out today, but I hope to have been understood on some of these points. I especially hope that I have not been understood merely on details. I would like to be understood on the far-reaching issue of our need to be in cordial harmony with the parent body if we are to function effectively in the Waldorf School. I particularly wanted to point out the need for this because it actually already exists to such a great extent, and we will be best able to find possibilities for progress in this area if the groundwork has already been laid.

Out of the details of our aspirations, which can be addressed in the discussion to follow, out of all the details that come up in these parents' meetings, let us take with us the impulse for cordial harmony among teachers and educators and the parent body. You parents certainly have a profound vested interest in this harmony because you have entrusted the most precious thing you have to the faculty.

Out of this awareness, out of our awareness of the faculty's responsibility toward what is most precious to the parents who are associated with us, out of this collaboration may the spirit which has showed itself in the Waldorf School to such a satisfying degree continue to flourish. The more this unity thrives, the more this spirit will also grow and thrive. And the more this is the case, the more we will also achieve that other thing, that best of all possible human goals: to educate the young people entrusted to the Waldorf School for their life in human society. These people will need to stand up to the storms of life. If they are capable of finding the right ways of working together with other people, then it will be possible to resolve the individual human and social issues.

From the discussion

A question is asked about the Abitur.

Dr. Steiner: I myself have only this to say: On the whole, the principle I have already presented applies. Through economy of instruction, we must get to the point where what we can achieve for the children at the most important stages in life will enable them to fit into what is demanded today. We cannot set these standards or decide whether or not we think they are right; we must submit to them. We are not being asked the question of whether or not what the *Abitur* requires is justified. This will have to be accomplished through economy, and as of now we are not yet in a position to do this, but I fully believe that it will be possible to achieve this goal, even though it does not yet look like it in the case of the people in question. Our principle, however, is to make the children able to take the exam at the appropriate age. But there are also external difficulties to be overcome; the school must be approached without bias. Naturally, I know that it would be possible for someone to flunk boys or girls even though we had brought them to the point of being able to take the exam. I gave you the example of how it would be easy for me to flunk the commissioners themselves. We are striving to have our students be able to take the exam, regardless of what we think of it. We want our teaching to be in line with real life and not with some eccentric idea. As much as possible, we must try to introduce our students to life in the right way.

Something along these lines is still possible in Central Europe, while in Russia that is no longer the case. We must be glad for what we have. If we introduce it to the children now, more will be possible in the next generation.

I am emphasizing explicitly that we are not crazy characters who say that our children are only allowed to do this thing or that. We will go along with what is asked for in the exams, even if we are not always in agreement with it. Meanwhile, we are still taking everything into account that we deem necessary for the sake of humanity's salvation.

Question: Would it not be possible to have school only in the mornings?

Dr. Steiner: There is always more than one viewpoint to consider in questions like this, isn't there? It has been said that instruction should take place between seven o'clock and one o'clock. Now let me point out some of the principles involved. In the question-and-answer sessions during my course of lectures at Christmas, the question of fatigue was raised, and I mentioned that the intent of our educational method was to refrain from fragmenting and dissipating the children's attention by having an hour of religion followed by an hour of zoology and so on. The point is to teach in such a way that the children's attentiveness can be concentrated. That is why a particular subject is taught for a longer part of the school day and over several weeks on end. This view is derived from specific knowledge of the nature of the child.

It was asked if the children do not get tired. I must draw your attention to the fact that in principle in our way of teaching we do not count on head work at all when dealing with children between seven and twelve years of age. That would be wrong. Instead, we count on the involvement of the rhythmic system and of the emotions connected to the rhythmical system of breathing and circulation. If you think about it, you will realize that people get tired, not through their rhythmic system, but through their head and limb systems. If the heart and lungs were to get tired, they would not be able to be active throughout an entire lifetime. The other systems are the ones that get tired. By counting on the rhythmic system during these years, we do not make the children as tired as they would get otherwise.

Thus, when experimental psychology investigates fatigue and states as a result of its experiments that children are so tired after three quarters of an hour that they need a change, this only proves that the teaching was done in the wrong way, tiring the children unjustifiably. Otherwise, the time limit arrived at would be different. The point is to conduct the lesson in such an artistic way that this kind of fatigue does not set in. We can achieve this only slowly and gradually, because new educational practices along these lines can be developed only gradually.

You see, ladies and gentlemen, it is possible to prevent the children from tiring to a very great extent by teaching in the right way. This is not the case with the teachers, however, because they have to work with their heads. And if we want to do the pedagogically correct thing and keep the instruction in the hands of one person, I would like to know what the teacher would look like who is supposed to teach from seven o'clock in the morning straight through until one in the afternoon. This is the main thing we have to consider. These teachers would be exhausted by ten o'clock if they had been teaching since seven, and it is not a matter of indifference whether or not we would continue to wear them out. That is not desirable, regardless of how much I might wish that the children from out of town would not have to make a two hour trip for one lesson in school. But that is the exception; it is exaggerated. Secondly, there are some things that must simply be accepted for the sake of achieving anything at all. Of course we cannot arrange the lessons for all the children in the way that would be desirable for the ones who live so far out of town. Of course that cannot happen. In such things, therefore, we have to deal with the actual circumstances.

In any case, we have arranged things so that the lessons that address the children in spirit and soul are given in the morning, to the extent that this is feasible. The afternoon is for eurythmy and artistic lessons. Instruction has been integrated into the times of day in a way that corresponds to the children's age and nature. It would be a mistake to hold school from seven o'clock in the early morning until one in the afternoon, and this mistake would arouse a great deal of discontentment. It would require a complicated and completely different system [of scheduling]. Then, too, I would like to see what would happen if we had the children in the Waldorf School from seven to one and they were left to their own devices for the rest of the day. I would like to see what kind of notes and complaints would come from home because the children were coming back from their afternoons with all kinds of bad behavior. We would have to deal with both sleepiness and bad manners on the part of the children. Add that to the sleepiness of the teachers, and those notes would be full of bad things.

There are several points of view to be considered. I appeal to you to consider as a matter of course that since we could not avoid having school in session in the afternoon, the reasons we took into account took precedence.

A father asks that the students taking the Abitur be tested by a committee of Waldorf teachers.

Dr. Steiner: This is actually not an issue of education, and our work is with educational impulses. The point for us is doing what I mentioned—taking into account what is in accordance with the nature of the human being and making sure that the children are not forcibly excluded from actual life. Given the way things are, there may be certain possibilities for us in the first years. But I ask you to consider that we are exposed to certain risks in assessing whether or not a child will be able to pass the exam.

What do you think would happen if we were to guarantee that no boy or girl who graduates from this school would flunk the exam? In some cases, the parents have anticipated that the child would have difficulties with the exam and sent him or her to us for that very reason.

As teachers attempting what I have indicated, we will continue to make progress toward the possibility of the children passing the exam. Those who do not wish us well, however, would be able to prove systematically that this is not the case.

It is not up to us to make sure that an officially certified commissioner is present at the exam. If the parents want the exam to be administered by Waldorf teachers, then the parents would have to take the initiative to bring this about. It is not something that is inherent in Waldorf education. This is an issue of opportunity that would also have to be resolved as the opportunity presents itself, and perhaps by the parents. It is not that we want to be excluded from issuing valid diplomas, it is only that we will have to look at the matter from the educational point of view. I would like someone to prove to me that it makes sense from an educational point of view to subject the students to a school-leaving exam when you have been together with them for years. I would like someone to prove that it makes sense. We know what we have to say about each of our students when they have reached school-leaving age. If this needs to be officially documented for other reasons, then that can happen, but it is not actually an educational issue. Those who have experience in this field know that we can tell what a student is fit for better without exams than with them. We have no reason to work toward the goal of being allowed to administer the exams because this does not follow naturally from what underlies our educational methods.

A question is asked about discipline and the attitude of respect toward the teachers.

Dr. Steiner: If you ask whether respect exists wherever Waldorf pedagogy is *not* being applied. . . . It is extremely important to have devotion or respect or love for the teachers come about in a natural way. Otherwise it is worth nothing. Enforced respect, respect that is laid down in the school's regulations, so to speak, is of no value in the development of an individual. It is our experience that when children are brought up in a way that allows their own being to set the standards, they are most likely to respect their teachers. This is no grounds for complaint. Of course it cannot be denied that some individual instances do not exactly give evidence of respect. It all depends on how much the respect that grows out of love is worth, and how much more the other kind is worth if it is only demonstrated to the teachers' face and not so much when they turn their backs. You must not imagine this as a situation in which each child does what he or she wants. It is a case of the children developing ever greater confidence in the faculty.

The progress in this particular respect is quite extraordinary. Anyone who is in a position to make the comparison will find that our progress with regard to discipline has been extraordinarily great in the past two years. The fact of the matter is that when we first got the children here, we had to think about how we would maintain discipline and so on. Now we have arrived at quite a different standpoint, actually. We have accomplished the most by having the relationship between teacher and child be a natural one. There is a great difference between how discipline is maintained at present and the situation a year and a half ago.

These things cannot be judged from a point of view that is brought in from outside; you must consider the Waldorf School itself. Respect cannot be beaten into someone—by which I do not mean to say that anything else can be. Respect must be won in a different way. In this regard, your apprehensions are understandable, but it is also necessary to break the habit of apprehension and look more closely at the results that are becoming evident in the Waldorf School.

If our school is still in existence after another couple of years, we will talk again about whether we have reached the point where our graduates can take the exams. Let us discuss it then. We are convinced that in principle this should be possible. By then we will also be convinced that there was no reason to fear that our method of education would bring about what is so very evident in the schools where compulsion is strongest, where I have seen in both the lowest and highest grades that things are in a bad way when it comes to respect. I do not think that we can take it as gospel that respect only thrives where there is compulsion in education, and that meanwhile our children are thumbing their noses behind their teachers' backs. If you deal with a child in the right way with a friendly warning, that is better than a box on the ear.

Address at the assembly at the beginning of the fourth school year

June 20, 1922

Dear children, dear boys and girls of the Waldorf School!

I am going to speak to the very little ones first. Dear children, you have not been to school at all yet, and for you things will be different now than they were before. If you look back a bit, you know that you used to get up in the morning and rub your eyes, and then you got washed and dressed and had something for breakfast. Then many of you saw how your father had to leave very early for work, and how your mother worked busily all day long. Perhaps you spent the morning playing; you could do what you wanted until lunch time. You went out in the street or in the yard or somewhere else; you could do whatever you liked. Then you had your lunch. You had already gotten hungry and tired. Your father and mother gave you your lunch, and then they had to go back to work. After that you could play again or do something else. You did not need to work yet. That is the way things went until suppertime. You had your supper, and then you went to sleep again. The next day was the same.

Now you have grown bigger, and your parents knew that it was time for you to go to school. Some of you were glad and looked forward to it. All of you will be glad to be in school, but things will be different for you. Now you cannot always run around or sit down wherever you like. Or if you are sitting with your friends, you cannot pull their ears or their hair. Now you have to come into the classroom where the desks are. It is crowded, and you have to learn something. Write that on your hearts, write it really well: You have to learn something. You have to sit at those crowded desks, and you cannot pull your friends' hair. You have to pay attention to what the teacher is saying. You have to begin to be well-behaved, to be good. But I hope you will like being good. Why do I hope that? Your parents had to work, and they had worries. You had no worries yet. Your parents had to work to make sure that you could live. If your parents hadn't worked, you would have had nothing to eat. You would have had to go hungry.

Each of you has more than just a head, you also have a heart—in here. There is something living in your heart that you don't know about yet. There is a soul living in your heart. It is something very different from your head. There is a soul living in each one of you. If your parents had not talked to this soul, but only to your ears, you would not have learned to speak. But you can speak, and speaking is something you do out of your soul. Your parents made sure that you became a human being. You will need to learn a lot more than you have already learned, and that will make you a real human being. Now you are just a bit human. You will become real human beings only by learning something—you can become a human being only if you learn how to work.

Your good teachers will teach you all this, and you should like your teachers. You can learn only if you love them. When you go into your classroom every day, think about the best way to love your teachers. If something hurts you or you are unhappy about something, then go to your teachers; think about how you love them, about how they will help you. Learn to love your teachers just as you learned to love your parents. Think about how your parents sent you to the Waldorf School. They wanted to do the very best thing for you. So do the best you can, too, by really paying attention to what your teachers are doing. That will show your parents that you love them, and they sent you to this school.

So, dear children, if you really come into your classroom in the morning with this feeling, and imagine that you need to grow up to be proper human beings, then everything will be fine, and you really will grow up to be proper human beings.

Now I would like to talk to the children who have already been in school, who have already learned how you begin to find more and more in your soul, in your inner person, and how you learn to really love your teachers more and more. This is what we have to promise ourselves again and again—to really love our teachers. Then we will be able to accomplish our very best.

Your teachers are always thinking about what they can do to teach you to grow up to be proper human beings. More and more, you must learn how to be children who work hard and pay attention, to be children who love their school. Your school is trying to teach you things that will make you good, capable human beings and good, capable workers for all the work humanity needs to have done. Here in this school, we are thinking more and more about what we need to bring to you, the students, so that you will be able to go through life in the best way. You have learned things that were all intended to teach you to be good, proper, capable human beings. If you work so hard and pay attention so well and love your teachers, your life will be different than if you are lazy and never learn to love your teachers. By taking in all that you can take in in school, you will become able to work for your fellow human beings, to be something of value to them.

The worst thing in life is for a person to lead a life that has no value for his or her fellow human beings. Then people don't want to have anything to do with you because there is no work you can do for them. What school gives us is finding a place in life that makes us able to do something for our fellow human beings, able to work for them, able to give them something of value so that they can love us for doing something for them.

People doing things for other people—that, my dear children, is what life is all about. We are constantly trying to get to the bottom of this here in the Waldorf School—how to guide children into life in the best way so that they will be able to do something for their fellow human beings, so that there can be joy in their lives and not just sorrow.

Those of you who are still in the middle grades can rely fully on your teachers. You can look up to your teachers. They are already fully involved in life. They have become people you can love, people from whom you can learn a lot. The best way to make progress is to tell yourself that you want to become like your teacher.

If I may still say a few words to those in the highest grades, I would like to say that you are now beginning to hear something that comes from a different direction. You do not yet know exactly what it is that you are hearing, but we will call it "the seriousness of life." When you get to be fourteen or fifteen, something of what we can call the seriousness of life is already coming toward you. It already resounds in your soul from time to time. In school you are presented with what you are supposed to learn, but when you have left school, there you stand in life. That is when your real life is supposed to begin.

What you should inscribe on your souls, especially this year, is to commit yourself to school, now more than ever. This school knows how to deal with the seriousness of life; it knows what to bring to children so that they can find their way into life's seriousness as they grow up. When we experience suffering, we must have the strength to bear it. We are meant to acquire this strength from what we gain in school. We must have the strength to bear life's suffering. But life also brings joys, and they are sometimes more dangerous because they make us thoughtless and dull our feelings. Here, too, school helps you learn to keep to the middle, to make your way between the joy and suffering in life.

Life today has become very complicated. Young people cannot always judge what they need in life or what will be useful to them. Your teachers are busy day and night trying to find out what life will be like ten or twenty years from now. You will need to love people in order to take your place in life in the right way. You know, my dear children, that I will never tell you at the beginning of the school year that you can learn here by playing. That is not true; it cannot be. There must be real seriousness here, so that you learn to take life seriously when it is hard to take. This seriousness will allow you enough time for human feelings. Here with us, this is supposed to go all the way up into the highest grades. You are meant to feel your way into what is really there in a human being. You must learn to understand that people have to learn by working, because if they do not, they cannot be real human beings.

It is now my pleasure to warmly welcome the teachers who have been here with you, who have already given you their love, as well as those who are working here for the first time this year. If every student knew what effort it takes on the part of the faculty, then love for your teachers would be a matter of course; it would be in the very air you breath here in the Waldorf School.

We are also trying to bring human beings into the right connection to the spiritual worlds. Our teachers have sought this connection to the spiritual world for themselves, and thus they will be able to be prophets and missionaries for you, transmitting what can only be brought into this world from the spiritual world. It is necessary for people to take this up and incorporate it into the earth as a spiritual force. Otherwise our earth would become barren. Here, through our loving and energetic work with each other, what makes a person a true human being is meant to awaken.

Now I would like to call to mind for all of you, especially the students in the upper grades, what we find out there in life. Our time in life is filled up with work, but now and then we stop working and celebrate certain festivals. At these festivals we remember what their value is for us: They give us enthusiasm. We must acquire enthusiasm in order to see beyond what each day brings. What is happening here today is meant to be a festival for you. When you enter a new school year, you who are in school and growing up should experience it as a festival that is incisive for your souls. You should tell yourselves to feel especially aware of the need to work hard and pay attention in school and to be connected to your teachers through love. You should experience something like a religious service in this and know that its forces are what illuminate and shape all of life. You should feel this to be something that is human in the highest sense of the word, as a special festival for your hearts, your souls, and your spirit.

Let us sense today what we have from being able to be in school to become real human beings. We will now begin working in school as proper, faithful human beings who love our teachers. This work is work for life. Today, with all our strength and out of the love that has been given to us, let us recall that human beings come into the world from the spirit, and let us promise to celebrate the festival of working in school, of a work that is carried by love.

If we have this awareness, we will work seriously; we will work out of love for our teachers; we will work in a way that allows what approaches us to enter our hearts. By being good students we will grow up to be good, capable people who will be the salvation of the other people in the world.

Address at the second official members' meeting of the Independent Waldorf School Association

June 20, 1922

After the points of business, Rudolf Steiner took the floor:

On the whole, it can be said that many of the outcomes of our goals actually constitute a single phenomenon within a larger framework of facts. Please allow me to make a few comments on this, and especially on the experience we have gathered since founding the Waldorf School.

As you know, we founded the Waldorf School as one part of the effects that were intended to proceed from a spiritual movement that is over two decades old. The Waldorf School would be inconceivable without this spiritual movement. In its particulars, the plan to found the school came from our dear friend Emil Molt at a time when there was a certain interest in great humanitarian questions because it was a time of such great need. Counting on this interest, we began to work in many different directions to try to influence aspects of public life from anthroposophical points of view. We may well say that since that time we have been able to acquire very extensive experience along certain lines.

To begin with, we encountered a certain interest that promised to encompass broader circles. In 1919 humanity had a great interest in working in one or the other direction to enable forces of ascent to replace the forces of decline that were so evident. And today we still see a universal interest in educational issues, not only in Central Europe but all over the world. It is a remarkable fact that this year's Shakespeare festival in Stratford actually took place under the auspices of educational issues. You know that I myself had to give lectures at this festival, and that the event stood fully under the sign of educational issues. In fact, a committee on new ideals in education organized this event. This summer we will have another opportunity to have a conference, this time at Oxford, where nine out of twelve lectures will deal with educational issues in a narrower sense.[8] This shows that at any rate an interest in educational issues is still present today.

This interest is to be found everywhere. In the widest possible circles today, we definitely find that educational issues are thought to be the most important issues of all. We find numerous people who believe, and rightly so, that any talk of social issues does not rest on firm ground if it does not take

8. This international congress on "Spiritual Values in Education and Social Life" at which Rudolf Steiner was invited to speak took place under the patronage of the English Minister of Education and others active in public life in England. From August 16–25, 1922, Steiner spoke on "The Basic Forces of Soul and Spirit in the Art of Education" [Die geistig-seelischen Grundkräfte der Erziehungskunst], 12 lectures, Oxford, 1922, GA 305, 1978], see *The Spiritual Ground of Education*, Garber Publications, Blauvelt, NY, n.d.

educational issues as its starting point. We have come to realize that the chaos that humanity has fallen into and will continue to fall into has essentially been brought about by our failure to place the right value on the spiritual issues of humankind's evolution.

However, this interest is "thought interest," if I may put it like that. The way in which this interest manifests clearly shows that we are dealing with some kind of thought interest. People organize conferences on education just as they organize other conferences today. They get together and talk about educational issues, and it cannot be denied that extraordinarily clever things are talked about at these gatherings. People nowadays talk with extraordinary cleverness. A large portion of humanity today is smart, and it is also the case that the majority of these very smart people like to hear themselves talk. This creates the best circumstances imaginable for holding conferences to discuss how to find ways out of these chaotic conditions.

If it depended only on conferences of this sort, we would be well on the way. Ladies and gentlemen, this is something we should consider very carefully. I have often stated that I am convinced that if twelve people or some other number of people would get together to undertake to establish an agenda for educating children in the best way, something extremely clever would come out of it. I say this in complete seriousness. When it comes to establishing an agenda for assembling the best pedagogical principles for dealing with children, the literature available today is excellent. What people are saying today in these conferences is literature. However, it all depends on accomplishing the work that is to be done on the basis of real life. People who establish agendas are never dealing with real life. In real life you deal with a certain number of students and a certain number of teachers; you deal with people. These people will do what needs doing; they will do whatever they can do.

However, in order to actually accomplish what is theoretically possible, we depend on having our hands free to do our work on a humanitarian basis. This brings us to the fact that nowadays the presence of a "thought interest" in great existential issues is much less important than the presence of the will to actually bring about the conditions that make a system of education such as this one possible. The remarkable thing about this is that while there is the broadest possible interest in the thought or the feeling that such and such ought to be, this is not accompanied by any real will interest. That no real will interest accompanies it is the reason why I call what it is our conferences deal with, "literature." Literature is what it actually is; it is not something that will be transformed into action.

One of the most important facts about the background of the Waldorf School is that we were in a position to make the anthroposophical movement a relatively large movement. The anthroposophical movement has become a large one. This is evident from the fact that difficult anthroposophical books go through many editions.[9] Interest springs up everywhere. This is a "thought interest," or even goes beyond thought interest to the extent that the people who come together in the anthroposophical movement also have a feeling interest in it, an interest of the heart. In all of our modern movements people are coming together with a mere "thought interest" that is transformed into a talking interest in those who are somewhat active. The anthroposophical movement gathers together those people who have an intense human need, a soul need, to make headway with regard to the essence of the human being. This is

9. For example, if paperback editions are included, in 1980 *Theosophy* was in its 30th German edition (164,000), *Occult Science* in its 29th edition (108,000), *How to Attain Knowledge of Higher Worlds* in its 21st edition (150,000), *The Philosophy of Freedom/Spiritual Activity* in its 14th edition (156,000) and *Riddles of Philosophy* in its eighth edition (31,000).

what things look like when we consider an interest in knowledge, a feeling interest, more theoretically. There are very many people today who realize that there is something here that can satisfy their spiritual interests. That is how it stands today, and I hope that its growth is guaranteed in spite of the scandalous opposition to it.

But what we are lacking are people who are not merely interested in the anthroposophical movement becoming as large as possible and bringing forth as much spiritual content as possible, but who are also interested in making this anthroposophical movement happen, in being coworkers in its coming about. There are extraordinarily few of them. We have many people who listen, many who want something for themselves, but we have extraordinarily few people who are coworkers in the fullest sense of the word.

You know, when our conference in Vienna was being organized, which was not a conference in the same sense as other conferences—the point of our conferences is for people to get together to receive something they can take home, while in other conferences everyone wants to get rid of what they bring from home—in any case, when this conference was being organized, there had to be workers there to get ready for it and bring it about, and there had to be speakers there. There are always a small number of friends who nearly have to run their legs off, work their fingers to the bone writing letters, and empty out their wallets. There are only a small number of them, the Waldorf teachers and a small number of others, and they are thoroughly overworked almost every month of the year because of their involvement. Actually, they are always terribly overworked.

But at the end of a conference such as this, even if it is as successful as the one in Vienna, we experience once again that although all the conditions are in place for our Waldorf system of education to expand, or something of that sort, the way these conditions come about means that the small number of active people get in over their heads. Again and again we have to be on the lookout for new coworkers. Perhaps not all of you will agree with me, but I would like to state my experience quite openly. As things stand today, I believe there would be a possibility of gaining plenty of members. I got the impression in Vienna that it would be possible to attract enough people who would become coworkers in the best sense of the word.

But—and here our general concern coincides with our concern for the Waldorf School—at this point we bump up against the fact that it is not possible to expand our circle of coworkers for the simple reason that we have no money. People everywhere have the means of supporting their coworkers, but this is only possible for us to a very inadequate extent. The main question is always how to offer people the means to exist when we disconnect them from their previous means. That is the fact of the matter. Today, if we want to move forward, we need a large number of coworkers. Those we have are simply not enough. Thus, what needs to be taken care of can be done only by exhausting the strength of the forces we have, and what can be done in this way is at most a tenth of what could be accomplished under conditions at present if we could count on a full complement of coworkers. After the Vienna conference in particular, we could watch the experience I have just described welling up.

Naturally this is not a question of an ordinary appeal to the wallets of those who are already members. That is not the issue. The issue, to put it very strongly for once, is that in recent times whenever we have appealed to the will, the matter in question failed.

In the end, the Waldorf School movement is connected to the threefold movement. The Waldorf School movement is conceivable only within a free spiritual life. The "thought interest" we met with at first has not led to a will interest. When the attempt was made to accomplish the deed of founding the World School Association as our only means of expanding beyond Central Europe, this attempt failed.[10] It was to have encompassed the entire civilized world. The attempt to rouse whatever belief people had that the educational system must change, which was what was being attempted in the World School Association, was a miserable fiasco. There is such a terrible feeling of being rebuffed when you appeal to the will. I do not say that I am appealing for money in this case. We are lacking in money, but we are lacking in will to a much greater extent. The interest that exists does not go very deep, otherwise it would extend to the right areas.

We were able to found the Waldorf School. Herr Stockmeyer[11] read the ruling,[12] the gist of which was that as of Easter of 1925 we will lose our first grade, and eventually the four lowest classes. We would hardly have been able to open the school at all anywhere else. In founding the Waldorf School, we took advantage of the right moment in which it was possible to do such a thing.

Whenever the educational system is at the mercy of universal schematization, we can point to strongly working forces of decline. We encounter them everywhere. We can point them out wherever what is laid down in the regulations for primary schools is taken to the last stage. In Lunatsharsky's school system in Soviet Russia, it has been carried through to its conclusion. People there are thinking the way we will think here when this is carried through to its conclusion and the full

---

10. See note p. 119.
11. A teacher at the Independent Waldorf School in Stuttgart.
12. See note p. 95.

consequences have been felt. The current misery in Eastern Europe is what comes of it when this way of thinking about non-independent schools finds its way into practice.

I am trying to speak today in a way that awakens enthusiasm, so that people feel the spiritual blood trickling in their souls and a large number of people who realize this will commit themselves, so that public opinion is aroused. Actually, I must say that at any point in the last twenty years when I tried to speak a language that appealed to people's hearts not only in a theoretical sense, but to the heart as an organ of will, what I felt, first in the Anthroposophical Society and later in other groups, always made me wonder, "Don't people have ears?" It seemed that people could not hear things that were supposed to move from words to action. The experience of the fiasco of the World School Association was enough to drive one to despair.

How do we think when we hear something such as this ruling that was read aloud? We think that perhaps ways and means will be found to push through the lower classes for a few years, after all. Even in more intimate circles, not much more comes of it than thinking, "Well, maybe the possibility will be there for a few more years." The point, however, is for all of us to stand behind it now. Education must evolve independently, as has been emphasized ever since 1919. There is no other way for this to become a reality than through general acceptance of what is offered by the members of our various associations, who are in full agreement that something like this should exist, and through them being joined by more and more people who will become active members. The will has to develop first!

I would like to tell you how my calculation goes: If numbers speak, we can say that we have no money. Having said that, we then collect money and fill the gap by the skin of our teeth.

However, we will also not get very far by this means. We will get further only by the means I intended in speaking of the World School Association. We must have an active faith that what is being done will really become a factor in public opinion. In order to maintain the Waldorf School and establish additional schools, we need a growing public conviction that continuing in the sense of the old school system will lead only to forces of decline within humanity. This conviction is what we need. We will move forward only when instead of merely establishing schools here and there for the sake of practicing some kind of educational quackery, we can make the breakthrough to deciding to take our educational principles to the public in a way that will make them a matter of inner conviction for parents and non-parents alike.

Please excuse me, but in a certain respect I really cannot avoid saying that I know many people will recognize the truth in what I have just said, but you only really acknowledge the truth of something by doing something about it! By doing something about it! This is why, above all, we must make sure that we do not found schools simply to an extent that lies within our existing means, which come from our branches and from wallets that are already empty. We must try to work for ideas and ideals so that an ever growing number of people is imbued with them.

In this respect our actual experience is just the opposite. The current issue of the newspaper for threefolding has just announced that in future it will be a magazine for anthroposophy. Why? Because the promising beginnings in understanding threefolding have petered out. Because, fundamentally, we must go back to the style we had prior to the threefolding movement. In spite of the fact that a lot has been said about threefolding, this is another case of being driven to despair when you talk with people. We need something to come of this; we need it to enter public opinion. That is what we need above all else if we want to make progress with the Waldorf School.

I must admit that I have been saying this for a long time. But just about anything else strikes a chord more readily than what I have said today. I would like to say that if I see what lives in people's will as mere faith—well, no one believes that mere faith, the mere faith that humanity can only be helped by having an independent system of education, will accomplish anything. But it would lead people who are still able to do so to support us financially, so that we would not continually be left empty-handed in comparison to other movements.

The anthroposophical movement is the basis of the Waldorf School movement. Even if it is set back by scandalous things such as are happening now,[13] it has within it the necessary prerequisites for life. A lot of associations are founded that have adequate monetary means but no inherent prerequisites for life. Associations are constantly being founded, and people have money for them, and yet they fail. If all the money that people spend today on unnecessary associations could be directed into our channels, then the reports would look different. Herr Leinhas[14] would have to report that our reserve fund is so large that we will have to try to invest it fruitfully.

I do not believe at all that the main thing for us today is our lack of money. What we are lacking is the will to assert ourselves in real life, to insist that the portion of spiritual life that we acknowledge as true be given its due in the world. What use would it be if I had claimed that our effectiveness in the past year was satisfactory in some way? But here, in a members' meeting, it is necessary to speak from this point of view. I am

13. The opposition to Rudolf Steiner and the Goetheanum.
14. Chief accountant of the Independent Waldorf School Association.

fully convinced that our Waldorf School can get as good as it can, but if we do not find the possibility of imbuing public opinion with our educational impulses, then all of our fancy arithmetic will not help us at all.

The will to convince everyone must be present in an ever-increasing number of people. In addition, the conviction must become widespread that for the salvation of humanity, it is necessary for something such as is present in embryonic form in the Waldorf School to keep on growing.

That is what I wanted to have said to that percentage of hearts in which the impulse of will is present. We can get very far if we only think about what it depends on: It depends on us using our will to really get public opinion to where it ought to be. That is what I needed to say.

From the discussion

I must add that a great number of parents have expressed the request that something be done by the Waldorf School to manage the relationship of the faculty to the parent body—what can the parents themselves do for the children? I would like to say that we will very soon be giving careful thought to how we can work in this direction. At parents' evenings, I myself will try to offer something along the lines indicated by these many signatures.[15]

We will try to do everything possible along these lines in the very near future.

---

15. The thrust of this request can be gathered from Rudolf Steiner's presentation on "Issues of School and Home" at the parents' evening on June 22, 1923. See pp. 190–202 of this volume.

Expanding our circle of coworkers can be achieved only if the circumstances of which I spoke become a reality. Something must first be done to shape public opinion so that more extensive work can be undertaken. Then it will be possible to do many things. But as long as what is growing on our grounds remains the secret of the members, we will not be able to move on.

A question is asked, among others, regarding the official ruling mentioned in the speech.

Dr. Steiner: It would not help us to file a complaint with the authorities. As many people as possible must be won over to the idea that such a school should exist. The authorities are doing the right thing if that is the law. It is a question of opinions gaining a foothold, becoming an effective force. There is something much deeper at stake. We must decide to interpret things ambitiously, to realize that what we think to be right must become the opinion of the public. The point is to get this idea into as many heads as possible. That must be accomplished so that as many people as possible change their view.

Dr. Steiner (in response to a suggestion): That does not come into question at all. Influencing public opinion is the only possible means of bringing the other methods up for discussion. To win over public opinion is the only practical way for us to go. We have not done so because there are far too few of us who believe in such a thing. I imagined that the World School Association would be promulgated in a certain way. If the monthly contribution could be one franc per member, we would be able to achieve what would have to be achieved by such an association. It would only be a question of individuals working in such a way that enthusiasm is present in their will.

Without doing that, we will get no further; we will simply manage to use up our last reserves. Even if we still find a lot of well-meaning members, it would be impractical to carry out. Even if something like that were to become a reality, we would only use up our last reserves. Our experience has shown most recently that it is necessary to attract the circles that are interested in what we are doing but are being kept away by the fact that the majority of the current membership feels the urge to keep the membership small.

May I still say that although we have established a certain level of contribution for membership, it is very good not to exclude anyone who is simply not in a position to pay the whole amount. Alongside the paragraph in the bylaws, let us remember among ourselves that people can also pay less.

1 9 2 3

Address at the monthly assembly
after the burning of the Goetheanum[1]

March 1, 1923

Dear children, dear boys and girls of the Waldorf School! At the beginning of this assembly, we saw some of your schoolmates give a very good performance in eurythmy. But when they performed this moving poem about fiery flames ascending to heaven, your dear teachers and I had reason to be very sad. You see, when eurythmy reveals something from the heart, we feel the content of the revelation more strongly. And now something like this always reminds us of the sorrow, the pain and the suffering that your teachers and I experienced together because of the terrible flames that destroyed the Goetheanum, our dear Goetheanum. Your teachers had often told you about this Goetheanum, and you had heard what a great pleasure, what an inspiration, what a refreshment for your teachers' hearts each visit to the Goetheanum was.

But then, my dear children, dear boys and girls, your teachers' hearts and souls are deeply comforted again; they can say

---

1. The first Goetheanum, a massive wooden building, burned to the ground on New Year's Eve of 1922-23. Rudolf Steiner wrote about this building in *Wege zu einem neuen Baustil* [Toward a New Style of Architecture], 5 lectures given in Dornach, 1914, publ. Stuttgart, 1957, and in *Der Baugedanke des Goetheanum* ["The Architectural Idea of the Goetheanum"], one lecture given in Bern, 1921, publ. Stuttgart, 1958.

from the very depths of their souls that when something as beautiful as today's assembly can happen here in school, it is a certain comfort to them. It is a comfort for them to see what they have been able to plant in the hearts and souls of their dear students, for this is something that belongs to them spiritually, and even though it demands great sacrifice and devotion, hard work and attentiveness on the part of your teachers, it is something that lasts. With these spiritual belongings it is possible to conquer any raging flame that reaches out to destroy the human heart. And in painful moments and in the nights they spend working, it is not only the Waldorf School itself, it is also what lives in you, dear boys and girls, that is the greatest comfort for those who guide you. And you can make this comfort grow by doing what you have to do with hard work and attentiveness and with love for your teachers.

Once upon a time there were two people who went for a long walk one Sunday. They walked over the fields in the glorious sunshine, and finally they went into the woods, where they rested in a beautiful place in the shade of the trees and talked to each other. They were very tired and had to rest for a long time, and while they rested, they talked. And it happened quite naturally—for these people were already old—that they came to talk about the joys and work and sorrow and pain in life.

And it happened that one of them said, "Oh, life does have its pleasures, too. It gives us so much beauty. I was once in a gallery, for instance, where I saw pictures by many painters, and my heart was glad. It was so beautiful and grand, my soul opened up."

And the other one said, "We must remember the things like that. But just think, my friend, what it would be like if you had not learned to enjoy pictures when you were in school. You would have walked right by those pictures without understanding them at all. My dear friend, we must so often think back to how school gave us what makes life pleasurable and valuable."

And the other said, "But you know, we don't need to go back that far. On this nice walk we took today, when we saw the birds flying in the air, our hearts opened up and we had to sing songs of joy. Would we have been able to do that if we hadn't been able to prepare our hearts for singing when we were in school?"

And a thought occurred to the other one: "We could have learned that later. But when you learn something later, it doesn't come so fresh from your heart."

And while they were lying there driving their tiredness away, one of them grew very uplifted and happy inside, and said, "Oh, Nature is so beautiful; there is so much to find in Nature. But you know, we can understand Nature better and better all the time. If we learned to imitate Nature in the poems we say, for instance." And since he was in a mood to have fun, he recited a poem for his friend that ended in "Cock-a-doodle-doo!" And they were glad, not only because they could hear the cock crow, but because they were able to be so full of life and feel all this, having learned to identify with what was out in Nature.

When you are sad, it is a comfort to think back on your time in school. You cannot help but realize that here in the Waldorf School your teachers are making an effort to shape your lives so that later, in times of joy and sorrow, your many vivid recollections of the Waldorf School will be a great comfort to you. And then you will have serious times. You will realize that you would not be able to live if you could not work. And we would not be able to work if we had not learned anything sensible. And now think about how your teachers are working so that you will be able to work and live in the right way later on in life. The men and women who are your teachers are thinking ahead to your later years. I want you to inscribe that deeply on your heart. When we have a beautiful festive assembly like the one today, we are sure in our hearts that all of you can learn for life's sake. And if you can say to yourselves while you are in school, "Now, we will try to learn not only what is pleasant for us, but also what is unpleasant," then even what is unpleasant will become a pleasure and a joy for you. Later on in life, the pleasure for which you once had to work so hard will come to you.

These are all things we always have in mind. Here in this school, we are meant to prepare a good later life for you.

Our oldest students have felt this, and it was a beautiful feeling, dear students in the upper grades, to hear you express how you feel in this Waldorf School, to hear you say that you want to stay here as long as you can possibly go on learning, that you want to be taught here in same the way in which you have been taught until now, right up to the point when you step out into life.

There are great difficulties involved in this, many obstacles to overcome. We will have to experience these huge obstacles personally. We will try to overcome many different obstacles in order to achieve what ought to be achieved. This may already have inspired hearts that will strike you down for your ideals. The background for this was Emil Molt's founding of this school.

Now, my dear children, dear boys and girls, here is something that I have always said to you: If you love your teachers, —and they have real love for you!—then your love for them will be the power that allows their best guidance to enter your hearts and souls. This is why I am not going to finish what I have to say. I want you to finish it. I want to ask you especially whether you will try to apply hard work and attentiveness to what you want, to your life's goals, while you are here. If, from the bottom of your hearts, you do want to apply these things, then finish the words that I have spoken to your hearts; then say to me... [the children shout to Dr. Steiner that they will do it.].

Address at the assembly at the beginning of the fifth school year

April 24, 1923

Dear children, dear boys and girls! [Dr. Steiner turns to the first graders and says:] Many teachers have spoken this morning. I am sure you know what a teacher is. A teacher is a good person. But we need to know why a teacher is a good person. You have already learned from your parents what a good person is. Good people have many qualities, but there is one quality they have in particular: Good people love children. Your parents are such good people because they have loved you so much. And because they love you, they are sending you to school here, where you will have teachers who love you.

What should you do if you know that a teacher is a person who loves children? What should you do then? The ones who have already been here can tell you that, so ask the boys and girls whether they love their teachers. [The children loudly shout, "Yes!"] You see, they love their teachers.

Your teacher will be your second benefactor. Just think, you will learn what that means. Just like your parents, who have been and still are your benefactors, your teacher will also be your benefactor. The older children have already noticed something of how the teachers love them. And the further you go into the upper grades, the more certain you will become that you can grow up to be a good and capable person only if you learn something real and if you learn how to behave in life.

Dear children, many of you will not know what it means to be really good, and some of you think being bad is better than being good. Even while they are still in school, the older students are noticing that they are getting closer and closer to "real life," as we call it, to having to find their way in life. They have a special reason to think about how you can never actually be a real proper person in life if you did not really love your teachers for being your great benefactors.

I want you to inscribe that in your understanding and your feeling, and also in your conscience. Just think of how deep-seated that will be later on in life if it is inscribed in your understanding, your heart, and your conscience. You will really be able to think about what school made of you if you can inscribe it on your souls in this way.

Now, you are all coming here after a time in which each of you had to remember that there are benefactors among human beings, and that ultimately Nature is also our benefactor. But the last few days reminded you of humanity's greatest benefactor, of the One who underwent suffering and death nearly two thousand years ago out of love for humanity, who gave the spirit to humanity through His resurrection. It was a time when you could remember this great benefactor of the earth and of humanity, the Christ. We are now entering the spring of Christ, of humanity's greatest benefactor.

But by looking up to Him, by feeling what the Christ is, we learn what other benefactors can be. And you see, the reason why your teachers will be such good teachers for you is that they have tried hard to get to know the Christ; they have tried hard to turn their feelings toward the Christ in the right way at Easter, in the spring. But that is what you should have in mind right from the very beginning—that your teachers are filled with the strength that comes from this greatest of all humanity's benefactors. Dear teachers, I know that I do not need to say this in any demanding way, but only as a fact: How you raise and instruct these children will really make them feel throughout their lives that the strength that enters your hearts through the Mystery of Golgotha makes it possible for you to be their benefactors.

Last of all I would like to turn to you parents, and to put it to you in a few words that you bring your children to the Waldorf School because you see something special in the being of the Waldorf School. This special character of the Waldorf School is not something to talk about now; we will do that another time. But I would like to briefly characterize the star we have chosen to guide our work, so to speak, as what is meant to flow into education and child-rearing as a result of observing the human being. This is meant to deepen the feeling of responsibility of all of those who work here in the Waldorf School.

That is why, dear parents, it should be especially emphasized today, as if we were taking a vow, that we are aware that the holiest of things has been brought here to us. We have nothing to offer in return except our deep feeling of responsibility. On one side we have what the teachers see in the parents' decision to entrust their children to this faculty; on the teachers' side is their intention to work devotedly, full of the responsibility and strength that is needed to make the children grow up to become what they should become in school. When we see this decision on one side and on the other the feeling of responsibility of a clear-sighted heart, we feel what this means; we see that the children who have come here are God's gift to the earth and that they must grow up to be proper human citizens of the earth.

It is the purpose of any school to turn the children of God into citizens of earth. This will be a conscious matter for us and we will do it in the best way it can be done, out of our feeling of responsibility. I especially want to have said this to the parents.

This is the spirit we are trying to work out of, the spirit that you, my dear teachers, are trying to work out of. I would like to ask you parents to look into our school in this spirit and find out whether we are really in a position to do what you expect of us. It will be the greatest possible satisfaction for us if those who look at what we are doing with understanding are satisfied that we are striving to turn children of God into citizens of earth.

Address at a monthly assembly

May 3, 1923

My dear children, boys and girls! It is always a pleasure for me when it is time to come see you here in school. As I was on my way here today, something strange came to me:

> Once upon a time there were two children who went for a walk on Sunday. When they were on their way home, each child had a bouquet of flowers. One child said to the other,

"*My* bouquet is so pretty!" The other one said, "*My* bouquet is prettier than yours!" They each liked their own bouquet better, but one of them really did not like the other one's bouquet. One child had a bouquet with some flowers that were full of sweet nectar, but it also had ordinary grass in it and even some ears of grain and some thistles. The other child's bouquet had only sweet-smelling flowers in it. So the child with the sweet flowers said to the other one, "You know, I don't like your bouquet with all those kinds of things in it!" But the other child didn't like the bouquet with just sweet flowers in it, either.

Now, dear children, how do you think the story goes on? What happened was this: The child with the bouquet with the grain and the thistles had a story to tell the other one. Listen to what that child had to tell:

Once I went out walking on Sunday, and I fell asleep outside and dreamed a dream. And what did I dream? I was lying in a meadow, and all the big and little animals came and were talking with each other. There was a very strange teeny-tiny animal, and a great big animal. The teeny-tiny animal was a bee, and the big one was a calf. And the calf and the bee were talking together. The bee said, "Calf, you don't understand anything about plants, but I know all about them. I know which plants are sweet, and those are the ones I suck the honey out of. Then I take the honey to the people, and they really love the honey. If I didn't fly to all the flowers that smell nice, there would be no honey for the people." And then the calf said, "You know, *I* couldn't live on just the flowers that smell sweet, the ones that taste so good to you. All the flowers you just fly over and ignore are the ones I have to eat, and if I didn't eat them, there would be no milk in the world. But without milk, people wouldn't be fed, and then there would be no need for honey because there wouldn't be any people around to enjoy it!"

That was how these two children talked with each other. And then the child with the bouquet of sweet flowers understood that there was something he had to learn. The other child had already learned the right thing from her dream. The child with the sweet flowers now understood that sweet flowers cannot be the only ones, that there have to be all different kinds of flowers that work together, and so now he learned to love the bouquet with all the different plants in it. And the child who had slept and dreamed could say, "Yes, that's what the calf said. There are your kinds of flowers and my kinds of flowers, but we need all of them, and that is why a bouquet that has all different kinds of plants in it is much more valuable and precious than one with only sweet flowers!"

Now, dear children, when you go to school, it is like taking a walk on a beautiful Sunday, and you are meant to get the very best that you can out of school to take with you into life. And if you can take along a bouquet of everything your dear teachers have taught you, this bouquet will give you great pleasure. But all the different flowers must be in it, not just the sweet ones! You must learn that you sometimes have to take in things that are not exactly sweet. If you work hard and learn seriously, you will notice that the bouquet you are able to take with you into your later life has not only sweet flowers in it, but all the things that are full of life, all the things your life depends on. Think about that, my dear children, and obey your teachers lovingly each time they ask you to do something difficult. Then when you leave school you will have the most beautiful bouquet to take with you into life, and you will like it best if it has all of life's different plants in it. Each memory of your time in school will give you the strength you need in life, because when human beings grow up, they gain the most beautiful forces for their life if they take a bouquet of that sort with them when they leave school. These are life forces that last until death and even beyond.

And now let me turn to the parents. I would like to assure you, as I try to do at every such opportunity, that I am fully aware of the confidence you place in us. We will also truly try to equip your children's bouquets with all the plants that are suitable and necessary for a healthy, hard-working and satisfying life on earth.

And to you, my dear teachers, I am heartily grateful for trying so hard to put together the bouquets for our children's later life in the right way.

This is why I expect you, dear children, to come to meet your teachers with everything they deserve for putting in so much effort on your behalf, and for working so zealously for you. By that I mean your gratitude and love.

I would like to say one more thing to you. They have told me that in addition to working hard, you can still make noise. I remember that I myself have sometimes heard you make noise.

And now I *want* you to make noise; I want you to yell so loudly that this whole room echoes with your words, "We love our teachers!"

[All the children shout enthusiastically, as loudly as they can, "Yes, we love our teachers!"]

Address at the third official members' meeting of the Independent Waldorf School Association

May 25, 1923

Ladies and gentlemen, dear friends! It is incumbent upon me to open this third official members' meeting of this association for an independent school system, the Waldorf School Association. It gives me great satisfaction to be able to welcome you warmly in the name of the Board, and I would also like to express my pleasure in the fact that you intend to discuss with us the future fate of the Waldorf School Association. Before we embark on today's official agenda, please allow me to preface the report from the Board with some remarks on the affairs of the Waldorf School and on the course of the Waldorf School movement as such, to the extent that you are involved in this process.

Just a short time ago, an extremely gratifying pedagogical and artistic conference[2] took place, at which the aspirations of the Waldorf School movement (actually, of any educational movement that does justice to the demands of the present and the near future) were graphically presented to an audience that probably included all of you as well as many other interested parties. For the moment, therefore, in speaking of the current status of the Waldorf School movement, it is only necessary to point to what came to light at this pedagogical-artistic conference.

----

2. In Stuttgart, April 25–29, 1923. See Rudolf Steiner's *Pädagogik und Kunst, Pädagogik und Moral* [Pedagogy and Art; Pedagogy and Morality], lectures and speeches, Dornach, 1978.

However, I would like to still allow myself the luxury of emphasizing a few things that were important for the basic tone of this gathering. We held this last conference at a time when, as I was able to make you aware, the will of the Waldorf School movement had been able to prove itself and demonstrate its spread, as was apparent from the fact that I myself had been invited to speak on the nature of this movement on the occasion of the Shakespeare festival in Stratford in 1922. As a result of this, the Waldorf School movement became known in England, and this in turn resulted in an invitation to hold the vacation lecture series in Oxford. This put me in a position to speak at some length in England on what the Waldorf School is actually trying to accomplish. These Oxford lectures then resulted in the founding of an English school association that will focus for the time being on transforming the Kings Langley School into a Waldorf School of sorts. It will also work to disseminate the idea of the Waldorf School in England. This demonstrates, however, that ideals and impulses that are inherent in the Waldorf School movement engage current interests in a very intense way. And here, too, the fact that a number of teachers from England visited the Waldorf School over a longer period of time at the beginning of this year shows how strongly this interest has taken hold in England in particular.

A further consequence of the spread of the Waldorf School idea was the course that I held in Dornach just a short time ago for a number of Swiss teachers and educators who organized it.[3] In addition to the Swiss teachers, however, seventeen Czech

---

3. April 15-22, 1923. See *Die pädagogische Praxis vom Gesichtspunkte geisteswissenschaftlicher Menschenerkenntnis* [Pedagogical Practice from the Perspective of Spiritual Scientific Knowledge of the Human Being], eight lectures given in Dornach in 1923, GA 306, Dornach 1975. *The Child's Changing Consciousness and Waldorf Education*, Anthroposophic Press, Hudson, NY, 1996.

teachers took part in the course. At this course in particular, it was evident that in the hearts of people involved in education, it is a matter of course that something such as what is being attempted by our school movement needs to come about. In everything you heard at this course in Dornach, you could really recognize the educational professionals' deep longing for something to enter the art of education that would aim very strongly at both spiritualizing the art of education and making it truly practical.

It is also very understandable that a quite specific feeling should have come up and been expressed by the participants in this last educational course in Switzerland. Those who experience strongly what such a course attempts to accomplish come away with a feeling of consternation; they feel overwhelmed. Now, I am only recounting what was expressed to me at the course in Dornach: Someone who was stating the view of many of the attendees said that the serious-minded among them were overwhelmed to see how little they were in a position to cope in their own souls with all the pedagogically necessary impulses that assailed them over a period of just a few days.

You can see that I then had to respond to this objection, which seemed totally justified to me. A thought such as this expresses what is present in many people today. Many people of the present day know perfectly well that some incisive intervention must take place if our system of education is to be able to meet the social demands placed on it and to extricate itself from the circumstances into which it has fallen. We really do not often take stock of how necessary an incisive reform of our educational impulses is. But if we think about it, we find that in their heart of hearts, parents and teachers are half-consciously or fully consciously convinced of the need for such incisive impulses to enter the system of education. Then people hear what we have to say. In fact, at the artistic and pedagogical conference, many people reached the point of saying, in effect, "All *that* needs to be done? How are we going to manage that? We get such a wealth of demands dumped on us in the course of just a few days;"—excuse me for expressing it like this, but this is a feeling I have often heard— "we come here with the best of intentions and leave feeling like a poodle that has been drenched with ideals instead of water. Our first impulse is to shake off what has been dumped on us."

As I said, this was actually expressed frequently at the last conference in Dornach. My response was, "Yes, certainly I can see that, but you need to keep in mind that people have had a long time to get used to the educational practices that are prevalent everywhere in schools today. They grew up with them and are comfortable with them. Because people always have only a few days available to devote to progressive impulses, everything we have to say to them has to be said in a few days. Under these circumstances, it is totally understandable that people feel dumped on. However, if it is possible for the suggestions that will continue to be made to arouse interest in these issues among ever broader circles, then we will also eventually be in a position to present what we have to say at a slower place. Then people would not need to feel overwhelmed."

This is proof that very intensive work is needed so that it will eventually be possible for us to actually set the pace that most people need, it seems, in order to grasp our ideas, rather than burdening people with them in the twinkling of an eye, as it were. I must point out that if this insight is taken as a starting point, then people would give us the opportunity to express ourselves more exactly and more slowly. So everything depends on a real interest in this issue of ours developing in ever broader circles. As things stand at the moment, the situation is very strange.

You know, we must keep in mind the inner process the Waldorf School movement has gone through in the four years of its existence. Naturally, the facts need to be weighed up in the right way. We now have around seven hundred students in the Waldorf School and nearly forty teachers. Years ago we started with fewer teachers and not even two hundred fifty students. The meaning of these two numbers—two hundred or two hundred fifty students then, and seven hundred now—is something extremely characteristic of the Waldorf School movement. They indicate not only a pedagogical and methodological, but also a complete cultural and social transformation of the Waldorf School movement, a real transformation. Depending on your taste, you can say either that it has found its feet or that it has been stood on its head; it does not matter to me. What I mean is the following: When the Waldorf School was founded, the thought among our friends was a social one. The intention was to found a comprehensive school of some sort, in accordance with the social impulses that prevailed at that time and that were surfacing in people's social thinking and feeling in 1919. The idea of the Waldorf School was conceived on the basis of social circumstances. And now neither you nor Herr Molt will take it badly if I put forth a risky hypothesis—which is of course to be taken with the famous grain of salt—of how this transformation has taken place. I will try to express it clearly.

Assume for a moment that Herr Molt had not been an anthroposophist, but simply one of the many philanthropic factory owners of that time. This was not the case, but we may suppose that it was. On the basis of the social circumstances of the times, he would still have conceived the idea to found a school, but the Waldorf School as it is today would surely not have come about. The Waldorf School as it is today came about simply because it was born out of anthroposophy—that is, out of the circumstance that someone who was not only a philanthropic factory owner, but also Herr Molt the anthroposophist, conceived the idea and turned to anthroposophy for help with the school's instructional methodology.

These are the cultural, historical and social factors. An idea characteristic of the times was realized with the help of anthroposophy, which was to provide the instructional methodology.

Now you see, over the course of time a transformation has taken place, and now a large percentage of the students we have today are here because of the pedagogy and methods that are cultivated in the Waldorf School. That the idea of the Waldorf School has expanded within the school itself is due to this pedagogy and these methods, so the original idea has been turned inside out. The original idea attracted the pedagogy and methodology that is used here. However, the Waldorf School is what it is today—and rightly so—because of this pedagogy and methodology. They were the main reason why parents who brought their children to us later on sought out the Waldorf School. Thus, in the course of these four years, an important development has taken place: Within the Waldorf School, a pedagogy and methodology born out of anthroposophy have come into their own.

And this pedagogy and methodology were what interested the people in England, what called forth the course in Dornach and so on. There is a specific pedagogical idea that is being realized in the Waldorf School, and that is what I have recently had to emphasize ever more strongly. The seven hundred students and the general expansion of the Waldorf School are due to the pedagogy and methodology that are practiced in the school. This is also demonstrated by frequent attempts to found schools on the example of the Waldorf School.

For me, naturally, what has become a reality here was the important thing from the very beginning. From the very beginning I conceived of the task of the Waldorf School as a purely pedagogical and methodological one, and in fact it has become apparent over time that wherever people were interested in the idea of the Waldorf School, this was because of its pedagogy and methodology.

Now there was a decisive interest in these various courses on the part of teachers and educators, but I must say that it has also been demonstrated in the longings of the parents. You know, the day before yesterday a number of parents from Berlin approached me again and told me that they had started small school groups in which they had offered instruction and tried to apply Waldorf School principles, but that now the government had come and would no longer allow it, so they had to send their children to the public schools. They asked whether it would not perhaps be possible to create a means of informing people by setting up a branch of the Waldorf School in Berlin. They thought that since it is still possible here, where things are administered more liberally, to not have the government intervening in the Waldorf School, it might also be possible in Berlin if a branch Waldorf School were opened.

I told them that it would not work, and that we needed to realize from this example that carrying out the idea of the Waldorf School is not possible without outreach into the broadest possible circles on behalf of the idea, which recognizes what thousands and thousands of people, or even more than that, are unconsciously wanting. These people basically want the same thing that is wanted here and simply are afraid to admit that they want it. And I still maintain that I did the right thing in issuing the challenge to found the World School Association once the model was there. I also still maintain that our task is not to get involved in all kinds of other experiments that pop up all over the place like quackery in the field of medicine, if I might put it like that—not real quackery, of course, but what is branded as quackery—but that it is more important to spread a real understanding of Waldorf education ever further and further. It must be spread ever further, and then the other thing will happen too.

You see, the Waldorf School is actually a challenge inherent in the evolution of education and in the relationship of educational evolution to the great ideas of culture and society. Perhaps it will be of interest to you if I draw your attention to how a turn-about in human feeling has occurred over a longer period of time, and how our thoughts have not caught up with it.

In March, 1792, there was an imperial chancellor in Central Europe for whom the task of educating the populace was merely a matter to be summarized as follows: "It is incumbent upon governments as a matter of course to disseminate the riches of the spirit, and in this just as in the enjoyment of man's other social affairs it is up to governments to form a national policing agency of a sort." This was spoken out of the feeling of concern for educational matters that was current at the end of the eighteenth century, when it was thought that the people had to receive directives from above with regard to the enjoyment of all social and human concerns, and especially with regard to administering pedagogical and methodological affairs.

And in the nineteenth century there was a person named Fröbel[4] who said already as a young man of twenty-three, "All experiments in the field of pedagogy, including those of Pestalozzi, seem to me to be something crude and merely empirical. It would be necessary to arrive at exact principles of instruction, just as natural science has exact principles." That was what Fröbel said.

---

4. Friedrich Fröbel, 1782–1852.

These two things, the pronouncement of the imperial chancellor Rottenhahn in 1792 and the passage from the letter by young Fröbel to his friend Krause, permit us an approximate characterization of what was alive at that time. The opinion prevalent at that time, which is still prevalent and must now be overcome, was that there was no need for further ideas on issues such as education and its methods; it was a matter of course to leave such things to the state. And the other idea was the sovereignty of the natural sciences: Whoever studied them and took them as their point of departure would necessarily discover the appropriate pedagogy.

Within both the current of subordination to the state and the current of science, it has become evident that we have reached a dead end in the field of education. Of course people had the best intentions in saying that it was necessary to establish a form of state policing in the field of pedagogy. Of course they had the best in mind, but that did not prevent the development of all the things that people now feel must change.

Educators are sighing to see things change; they say that they do not know how they ought to be dealing with human beings, that they believed that the art of dealing with human beings could derive from a—I cannot call it a mishmash, since that is not how the adherents of exact science would talk, so let us call it a synthesis simply to use a different word—a synthesis of anthropology, psychology, and ethnology. More recently, psychiatry is also being included. Time has shown that what Fröbel wanted is not acceptable to a deeper feeling for education. In all the people attending the courses, in the wish for a branch Waldorf School in Berlin, it was evident that people are certain that something has to happen, but when Waldorf school people talk to them about things, they are like poodles drenched with the water of ideals. It cannot work its way into their heads in a few days; nevertheless, they know that something has to happen.

We must keep clearly in mind that our efforts correspond to the desires of thousands and thousands of people, and that we must do everything we can to make the idea of the Waldorf School and all its impulses become ever more popular, so that people begin to see it as a challenge of our times. All this needs is to awaken in many people the courage to recognize and act on what they have long experienced in their heart of hearts in an indefinite way. It has still been my hope recently that this would flow into the hearts of the friends of the Waldorf School ideal who come to gatherings such as this one, because this is the most important thing we need—to have the interest spread, to have the efforts to popularize the Waldorf School spread. This is what we need.

And you know, something similar is necessary with regard to our method's inner progress. When we founded the Waldorf School four years ago, we had eight grades. It was clearly apparent to us that we had to work out of a striving that had remained unconscious to Fröbel and his ilk, that we had to create our curricula and educational goals on the basis of a true understanding of the human being, which can only grow out of the fertile ground of anthroposophy. Then we would have a universally human school, not a school based on a particular philosophy or denomination, but a truly universally human school.

The ideal that had been hovering over people for centuries was clear to us then. Since we had to take other existing circumstances into account, we had to accept compromises, but only to a certain extent: The first three school years would have to be allowed to run their course in a way that derived its standards for instructional goals and curricula only from the teachings of human nature itself. Upon completion of grade six (at age twelve) and grade eight (at age fourteen) we would try to have the children at a point where they would be able to transfer to other schools. We wanted to create the possibility of making the Waldorf School ideal a reality for as long as possible, on the one hand, and yet still offer the children the possibility to transfer.

This is something that is actually easier to carry out with regard to the eight primary grades than it is for the expansion of the school into grades nine through twelve, which has also become necessary. To the primary school education we offer, we need to add college-preparatory and vocational high school education. People are now saying that we need to get these young ladies and gentlemen to the point where they can pass the *Abitur* and enter a college or university. (Although the good will is there among certain individuals to open an institution of higher learning ourselves, this is a huge illusion for the time being, and the things we cultivate must always rest on real and solid ground.)

Naturally, there are inherent difficulties in our needing to prepare the young ladies and gentlemen who graduate from this school to take the *Abitur* so that they will be able to attend colleges that will grant them the degrees they need in what is now called "real life." It immediately becomes apparent that in the upper grades, it is much more difficult to cope with both the challenge of the Waldorf School ideal of deriving educational goals and curricula from human nature itself, on the one hand, and the coincidental curricula that include nothing of what human nature demands, on the other.

When these young adults are fourteen, fifteen, or sixteen years old, we would really need to be introducing them to real practical life, which means that they should understand something of what happens in real practical life. But instead of that, along comes the teacher of Greek and Latin, reproaching us for trying to incorporate real demands based on understanding the human being, for including lessons in chemical and technological subjects, in weaving and spinning—in short, in things people should know about in real life. Along comes the Latin teacher, complaining of not having enough time to prepare people for the *Abitur.*

This is how these unsolvable conflicts arise. On the one hand, we are trying to make the idea of the Waldorf School a reality in the best and purest way possible, and on the other hand we have to break this up with all kinds of compromises that are imposed by the fact that we are not allowed to tear the young people away from so-called real life, if you will excuse the expression. If we help them find their place in life as they should, they are rejected by so-called real life and become bohemians. (I used that word recently in the course in Switzerland and immediately had to apologize because some of the participants were from Bohemia.) The fact is, however, that we must come to the fundamental realization that we are not striving for bohemianism as an ideal, but for a really practical life, for a way of teaching and raising children that gives people a firm footing in real life. But before we can do this, an understanding of what human nature really encompasses and demands must become as widespread as possible.

Thus, we will not popularize the idea of the Waldorf School without first deciding to make understandable what I have pointed out today. In broader circles we will not popularize the idea of the Waldorf School if we speak only of abstract things, of having the children learn comfortably and through play and so on. If we present the same trivial thoughts that others also present, if we do not go into the concrete things that really lie dormant in people's hearts, we will not succeed in popularizing the idea of the Waldorf School.

Today we are faced with the difficult task of having to do something so that in future we are not always living from hand to mouth with regard to the Waldorf School's finances. Given the existing state of the finances, we never know whether we will be able to sustain the school for three or four months into the future; we are forced to economize with no end in sight. Of course it is true that the idea of the Waldorf School gives us such a firm footing that we can also summon the enthusiasm to go on into the unknown. On the other hand, however, responsibilities do arise. Actually, hiring each new teacher is such a responsibility that it really needs to be said for once that financing the Waldorf School, which is the point of departure of the Waldorf School movement as the first pedagogical example of how to raise and educate children according to this method, would have to rest on foundations that guarantee a certain measure of stability.

That is what I wanted to add as the necessary consequence of what I said before, so to speak. This august body would need to apply every means available to come to decisions that will make it possible to stabilize the financing of the Waldorf School at least to the extent that we know we will be able to carry the responsibility for it, and that it will never get to the point where the whole thing falls apart in a few months. We see the factors involved in taking our cause to the world in a financial sense. If this would happen, the outer framework would be there too.

Ladies and gentlemen, dear friends, I can assure you that the things we experience in courses such as the ones I gave at Oxford and in Switzerland, the things we experience as the longings of teachers and parents, show that the Waldorf School movement is a challenge that is deeply embedded in the evolution of our civilization. This is proved in practical terms today by what has gone before. On the other hand, our ways of working in the Waldorf School, the fact that there is actually something present in the college of teachers, gives evidence of something from which the entire Waldorf School impulse radiates. It demonstrates how a strong will is making itself felt in the world out of the purest possible enthusiasm, as may have become evident to you most clearly during the recent artistic and pedagogical conference. In these two aspects, I might say, the school stands on firm foundations. Please excuse me for asking you to consider ways in which these two pillars which I have particularly tried to characterize, the first pillar of the challenge of the times coming from parents and teachers and the second pillar of the sacred, expert and fully appropriate enthusiasm that lives in the Waldorf School, can be joined by the third pillar of stabilizing the school's financial foundations.

It is sad to have to speak of this. However, the fact of the matter is that doing anything at the present time takes money, lots of money. We can be certain that if we find ways to awaken understanding for the impulse of the Waldorf School, we will also arrive at the necessary financial means. This is why we must find the way from the first part of what I presented to what I have so presumptuously—there is no other word for it in this case—added to it by way of conclusion.

Points of business followed.

Address at a parents' evening:
Issues of School and Home

June 22, 1923

Ladies and gentlemen! For a long time we have been aware of your active wish to have the issue of school and home, children and parents, discussed here at a parents' evening.

It is not possible to say everything there is to say on this subject in one evening, but we will continue to organize evenings where these questions can be discussed so that the topic can be covered exhaustively. Today I will articulate the basic main points that the teachers and I have in mind.

In the field of education, parents' evenings are often proposed, but many representatives, even outstanding ones, of today's official school system do not think much of such parent's evenings. Some excellent educators say that nothing comes of them except fruitless discussion. Now, different points of view are possible with regard to everything in practical life, including parents' evenings, and there is some foundation for all of them. I will not dispute people's right to think little of parents' meetings from their particular point of view. We, however, as representatives of the idea of the Waldorf School, must see something of extraordinary significance in these parents' evenings, because if these meetings can be conducted in the right way, they are connected to the conditions most necessary for the life of what we intend to bring about through the Waldorf School.

To be sure, teachers who have found their place in the social context that is prevalent today, who feel supported by state authorities, are at home and secure in this and are very often satisfied with it. There are plenty of people telling them what to do, so why take it from the parents, too? This is how they look at it.

This cannot be our point of view. We are not embedded in current societal circumstances in the same way. We have to work out of the guiding light of our understanding of human beings and of life, out of human science and human art as our pedagogical goal. As educators, we must draw what we need for our teaching on a daily basis from the inner strength of our hearts. For that we need, not recognition—I do not want to say that because an idea that derives as strongly as ours does from the challenges of the present and the future must be self-contained in the strength of its effectiveness and not count on recognition—but understanding; above all, the understanding of those on whom so much depends, of those who entrust their children to this school.

Without this understanding, we cannot carry out our work at all. This understanding must be general in nature at first. We cannot claim to be guided by a higher wisdom, derived from the acknowledged social order and hovering above our heads, and to need nothing more than awareness of this wisdom. We must gain leverage for the ideals of our school, and this happens when people see that what comes to light through the idea of the Waldorf School is very deeply rooted in the most important cultural demands of the present and the near future. Therefore, we must strive to present our intentions to our contemporaries in a clearly understandable form, in a form that can engender understanding. Above all, we count on the understanding of those who entrust their children to us, who therefore have a certain love for the Waldorf School. We count on them being able to grasp the thoughts, feelings, and will impulses that sustain us.

Thus, we would like first and foremost to establish a relationship between the school and the parents that does not rest on faith in authority. That is of no value for us. The only thing that is of value is having our intentions received with understanding, right down into the details. The only thing that is of value is the awareness that this school is taking a great risk in trying to use feeble human forces to recognize the scarcely decipherable demands of the twentieth century and to recast them in the form of an educational venture. I believe there is no single member of our faculty who is not trying to experience what we are involved in as some kind of solid footing in world history, in humanity's evolution. This is what our teachers are trying to do in all modesty. As necessary as modesty may be, however, we must not be timid in what we are doing. We must be aware that what we are doing is significant, but also that this significance rests not in our own character but in what we acknowledge to be true. The significance of what we are doing must be looked at in the right way, not from an arbitrary or sympathetic standpoint, but from the standpoint of a will that stems from the consciousness of the times. This, above all else, is what we need from the parents.

We would like the parents of the Waldorf School children to say, "We are especially aware of our duty to educate human beings, and we would like to have our children make a contribution to humanity's great tasks in the twentieth century. We want entrusting our children to the Waldorf School to be a social act of some consequence." The more strongly this becomes a part of your whole attitude, the better.

We have to depend on your attitude above all else. We cannot think much of detailed guidelines on how teachers are meant to act toward the parents and vice versa. We cannot expect much from these guidelines, but we can expect a great deal from meetings between teachers and parents that take place with the right attitude, because we know that when people's attitudes relate to their inmost being, the attitude turns into action, right down into the details of life. When an attitude takes hold of a person on a general level, then his or her individual actions become copies of the broad strokes of the attitude's intentions. That is why it is more important for us to feel and understand the right thing in the right way than to lay down or follow specific guidelines.

I have emphasized how the different stages of life affect children, how children are different before the change of teeth than afterward, in the period between the change of teeth and puberty. Up until the change of teeth, children's destinies actually keep them in very close contact with their parents and their home. If we are not totally caught up in the materialistic way of thinking that is flourishing at present, if we can see through to the spiritual context within human interactions and evolution, we know that the destined relationship between children and parents is much greater than our abstract age with its materialistic ideas often assumes. If, in addition to knowing what physical life provides, we know what is given to us by life in the spirit beyond the boundaries of birth and death, then we take the destined relationship between children, parents and siblings very seriously, and the way in which children come into elementary school from home, which is really incisive for all of education, acquires significance for us.

Although this first part of my remarks may be somewhat far from the thoughts of most of you parents, it still seems important to me to touch on this. Those of you who already have children with us may have younger children at home. You may have come to love the principles of the Waldorf School and want to send your younger children here too. For you, tonight's subject of raising pre-school children will be important.

On entering school, children are true reflections of all the characters and circumstances in their parent's home and in their environment as it has been until now. Up to the age of seven, children are almost entirely sense organ. They take in everything from their surroundings with incredible sensitivity—everything that is said, done and even thought. Hidden within this is a secret of human growth that is largely disregarded by today's science: Expressions of soul in a child's surroundings are transformed into the child's organic, bodily constitution. Anyone who has acquired the educator's fine feeling for a child's appearance that a Waldorf teacher is meant to have will see by the shine in a new elementary school student's eyes whether that child has been treated lovingly at home or has been treated unlovingly and subjected to outbursts of anger in his or her environment. What parents and siblings and so forth do, say, and think lives on in a child's bodily constitution. If I wanted to, I could say a lot about how these expressions of soul can be observed in the processes of breathing and blood circulation and in the working of the child's nervous system. Due to certain circumstances, the child's father and mother may tend to have frequent outbursts of anger in dealing with the child. In such children, we notice what they have taken in and bound up with their inner being. It has turned into their bodily constitution; it is there in how their digestion works, how their muscles move, and even in how they can and cannot learn.

It is literally, not figuratively, possible to say that when a first-grader is entrusted to a teacher, the teacher receives a complete image of the parents' home. In their health, temperament and ability to learn, children bring their home right into school. Our first intimate acquaintance with the home is through the child. This should become part of the attitude of those of us who have a real interest in schools such as the Waldorf School. Such things need only turn into an attitude to begin to affect our actions.

When you are clearly aware of something like this, you will do some individual things that you would otherwise not do and refrain from doing many things you would otherwise do. This is no abstract knowledge; it saturates your whole life. If this prerequisite is present, it will result in the will to bring parents and teachers together in the right way. When we know that what is important works in the depths of human nature, we pay less attention to *what* is actually said in words in five minutes, but much more to *how* it is said. When the attitude I indicated brings parents to school again and again to encounter their child's teacher, the simple fact that parents and teachers are not strangers to each other but have seen each other before will start to bear fruit.

In this relationship between parents and teachers, what we need above all is for this interest in the generalities of Waldorf education to carry over to all aspects of school life, to everything that is connected to the Waldorf School through the faculty on the one hand and the parents on the other. If we know that at home there is a daily interest in what we as teachers are doing in the Waldorf School, then we can teach with a great feeling of reassurance, with a strength that gives us new incentives each day.

I do not deny the difficulty of mobilizing such interest. I am well aware that under current social conditions people have little time and energy to ask "How was it? What did you do?" when their children come home from school. I know that the children cannot expect their warm enthusiasm to elicit this question. The point is that parents should not ask this question out of a feeling of duty, but in a way that makes the children want to be asked. We should not be at all embarrassed that the children may sometimes tell us things that we ourselves have forgotten; that goes without saying and will pass unnoticed if the right enthusiasm is present on both sides. Do not underestimate this: If teachers can know that what they are doing sparks lively interest at home, if only for a few brief minutes, then they know that their work rests on a firm foundation. They can then work out of an atmosphere of soul that can have an inspiring educational effect on the children.

This is the most effective thing we can do to combat what has been termed by some of today's outstanding educators, "the war between parents and teachers." That is what they call it when they are speaking among themselves. This war is a subject of secret discussion among many educators. It has led to a noteworthy expression that is becoming well-known; young teachers in particular tend to use it: "We have to start by educating the parents, especially the mothers." We here, however, have neither the ambition nor sufficient Utopian sensibilities to do that. Not that we believe that parents are not educable or refuse to be educated, but rather because we want there to be a really intimate relationship of friendship between parents and teachers, a relationship based on the matter at hand. The parents' interest in the school can do a lot to bring this about.

While the parents' souls have very strong effects on their child's bodily constitution, it is only possible for teachers to work on the child's soul through soul means. Here, in place of the imitative nature with which a child encounters his or her parents before the change of teeth begins, there appears the principle of a necessary and natural authority. This is something we must have, and teachers are especially supported in this if an interest such as I have described is present. Much of what the parents can contribute to supporting this authoritative strength, to enabling their child's teacher to be the authority that he or she must be, can have its source in something as simple as the fact that school is taken seriously, with a certain ceremonial seriousness. A lot of sifting out goes into choosing teachers for the Waldorf School, and they are people you can have confidence in. And if you do not understand something, rather than wrinkling your nose at it right away, it is important that you trust in the great overriding principle in which you yourself believe. Then you will be supporting your child's teacher and making use of the opportunity to bring about a relationship of trust between parents and faculty.

You know that we do not issue report cards with grades as the public schools do. Instead, we try to describe what is typical of each child and to enter into his or her individuality. First of all, if teachers sit down to formulate reports and are aware of the responsibility involved, then riddle upon riddle appears to their minds' eye, and they weigh up every word they write down. It is a great relief to them in this process if they have actually met the child's parents, not simply because this tells them about the hereditary circumstances, which is all materialism is concerned with today, but because it allows them to see the children's environment, and then everything begins to appear in the right light. It is not necessary for the teachers to judge the parents themselves in any indiscrete way; they simply want to meet the parents in a friendly manner. Just as writing a letter to someone you know is different than writing to a stranger, it is also different to write the reports of students whose parents you know and those whose parents you have not met.

Secondly, the teacher should actually be able to know that such reports spark loving interest at home, and I believe that if parents would manage to write a brief response to what the teacher wrote in the report, it would be an incredible help. It would make no sense to institute this as a requirement, but it is extremely important from an educational standpoint if parents begin to feel the need to do this. Such notes are read with extreme attentiveness here in the Waldorf School. Even if they were full of mistakes, they would be much more important to us than many currently acknowledged accounts of modern culture. They would permit us to take a deep look into what we need if we are to teach, not out of abstract ideas, but out of the impulse of our times.

You must not forget that Waldorf teachers educate out of an understanding of the human being that does not come about in today's customary ways. A powerful human understanding would flow in what the parents could communicate to the teacher in a devoted way, and I do not exaggerate at all when I say that a response to a report card would almost be more important for the teacher than the report itself is for the child.

Here too, however, I place more value on parents maintaining a lively interest in everything going on in the school than I do in this specific measure I have chosen as an example.

Thus it is my opinion that the right thing will happen in the time the children spend on vacation if the school year runs its course in the way I have indicated. We would do well to let the vacation be a vacation and not pin the children down to doing anything school-like. However, if you can make the attitude I wished for into a reality, that would mean the right kind of happiness, joy, and healthy refreshment for your child.

We are particularly dependent on an atmosphere that is steeped in this attitude, so that you realize that the Waldorf teachers are concerned about every aspect of your child, including first and foremost his or her health. We are particularly concerned about being informed in our souls of subtleties with regard to the state of health of the children who are entrusted to us. An art of education is not complete unless it extends to this degree of interest in a child. This is an area, however, in which the work we need to do will be possible only if parents and school work together in the right way. We would like to see our school met by an understanding that arises from an inner need. We would also like to see the parents turn to the school for tips on their children's bodily well-being, diet and so forth. Above all we want to see the fundamental impulse behind our activity in the school, namely deep, inner human honesty and openness, take full effect in these details in the interaction between parents and teachers. This could lead to great results in life, and much can be done better in this regard if fathers or mothers come to the teachers and say, "My children are coming home from school tired; they get home too late. What can I work out with you to counteract that?" Working things out in this frank way can be the basis for many good things to happen.

In particular, it can help the school a lot if the parents lend their support in things in which exactitude, but not pedantry, is needed. It contributes a lot to how we can maintain order in the school and create a mood of seriousness among the children if everything about how children and parents interact in the morning makes it a matter of course that the children leave the house at the right time and therefore arrive at school at the right time, without any special commands being issued. Here, too, it is not so much the individual instances I am referring to as the consciousness that stands behind them, the attitude that school is something serious and ceremonial and that when your teacher is satisfied with your punctuality, you satisfy your parents as well. This is a moral note that the children bring from home each morning. A child's state of mind on leaving the house in the morning is not merely a source of satisfaction or dissatisfaction to the teacher's educated eye. Disturbing or supportive impulses find their way into the teacher's mood, too, if the child leaves the house in one way rather than another. Such things need to become conscious. I believe it is of no small significance for the rest of your life to have heard as a small child from your father, "There are two things that need to run exactly on time, you know—the clock, and getting children to school." Saying that now and then does not take much time, but it will have an effect on the rest of your child's life.

We are not dependent on details, but rather on a heart-to-heart relationship between school and home. We are confident that if this real heart-to-heart relationship is present, the right thing will come of it. We long to see this attitude awakened not merely with regard to details, but in full force. Then the Waldorf School will accomplish something not only through its cultural consciousness but also through such things as we have discussed today.

We must be clear that in our times certain innovations have been necessary so that deficits in such things do not come to light too strongly. Just think of what kindergartens sometimes have to do to make up for what has been done badly at home! Our times have become such that they require surrogates for what should be experienced in the family.

What we are trying to accomplish in the Waldorf School is something that needs to be followed not only intellectually; it must also be loved. And if the parents' attitude is steeped in this love, we will not need to raise our children in fear and in hope, which are the two worst but most used means of educating children today. The best means of educating children, however, is and always has been love, and home can be a great support for a school whose art of education is sustained by love.

Some people say that the discipline in the Waldorf School is not as good as in other schools. Time is too short to speak about this in detail now. Simply keep in mind that things have changed a lot in recent years, not only in society but also in the souls of children. We cannot apply the standards of our own youth. There is a deep gap between the young generations of today and the older ones, and when getting an educational grasp on the being of a child is at issue, we will do badly if we educate on the basis of fear of punishment and hope for good grades, but we will do well if we teach out of love. No matter what kind of wild turmoil is going on in the classrooms, if children have the right relationship to their teachers, if the children are still able to see in their teachers what they are supposed to see, then all their boisterousness will not mean what it would mean otherwise. This may be paradoxical, but it is psychologically correct. We begin to look at boisterousness in a different way: The children are getting it out of their systems so that it will not have to come out later on, which is decidedly better than the other way around. Later stages of life are based on what we foster in school, you see. If we are deeply convinced that we are educating with a whole lifetime in mind and not just for the current moment, then we also know how much we need you parents in order to move forward with the idea of the Waldorf School.

These are the points of view I wanted to present first. I want to emphasize that they contain what is most important, and that we will get very far indeed by taking hold of them honestly and thoroughly. This will also strengthen the Waldorf teacher's sacred conviction, with which we hope you agree. We know that we will achieve our goal if the school's intentions are understood at home and if it is made possible for us to work together intimately with the parents.

1 9 2 4

Address at a monthly assembly

March 27, 1924

Dear children, dear teachers, and dear parents who are here today! Each year when Easter comes, it is a very special festival for the school, a special festival for children to experience and a special festival for all of human existence. This festival is anticipated in the beautiful language that nature now begins to speak to us.

Of course nature is always beautiful, and anyone who is sensitive to it can find beauty in it even in winter, when the snow makes its way up the mountains and covers the ground and the trees in a way that is almost sad. It is beautiful then, too, but it is cold outside, and that makes our souls cold and reminds us of how often life chills our hearts and souls.

But then in spring, as Easter approaches, the seeds sprout and the flowers spring up out of the ground. The March violets are a greeting from the sunlight and the world-spirit itself. And the green reminds us of our hopes in life, of what we wish to have from life. The color of hope, of wishing, and of joy in life is there in the green.

Turning from nature to our school of life, because we must say that a school of life is what the Waldorf School intends to be—and now I am speaking to you, dear children—the fact that life is now beginning to unfold outside makes Easter a festival that has a great effect on the school, on the children and on the teachers and on the parents, who are the most important thing standing behind the school's children and faculty. At Eastertime, the new children enter our school.

This is when the teachers see the life task they face in educating these new children. This is when a wonderful soul-relationship has to come about between the teachers and the parents who are entrusting their children to them. At Eastertime, for a number of children and teachers, something begins that will continue for years as these teachers grow close to these children whom they love so dearly.

But at the same time, there is something different associated with Easter. It is also the time for graduation from school, as is now the case with us for many of the eighth graders and all of the twelfth graders. This is the time when their teachers are heavy-hearted, because they have grown close to these children in soul and in spirit. It is also the time when we can see the heavy hearts of the children who must now leave this school, which was a preparatory school for life, a school where everything possible was meant to be done to show the hopeful side of life. They must now leave this bright, beautiful summertime of their lives and go out into an existence that is often raw and hard, where there is so much pain and so many joys to experience. Life has a lot to give us—joy and sadness and problems—and we must cope with it. And when the festival of Easter is approaching, as it is now, when we turn our gaze to the coming of Easter, we are reminded of how this festival is a very incisive one in the hearts and minds of students and teachers.

In welcoming their new students, teachers look toward everything that is to come. They feel their tasks as teachers especially strongly now, as they turn to the parents of these children and realize that these men and women are showing their confidence in them by bringing them their nearest and dearest. This is something meaningful that should enter the teachers' hearts and be very deeply felt. The children come in, joyfully looking forward to what they will be graced with through their teachers love and through everything that human beings have brought forth.

Then we must also be aware of the departures, for one or the other student will have to leave this school. That is when we get the other feeling, a feeling of mixed wistfulness and sorrow in many respects. Especially for teachers, this engenders a very wistful sorrow in their hearts and minds, because they must now send the children they have grown to love out into life. These children must now seek for themselves what they and their teachers had sought together in school. But to this is added the satisfaction of being able to say as a teacher, "If you have succeeded, then they will take with them the strengths that you wanted to give them." This thought is what makes graduation beautiful for the teachers and makes their Easter a happy one.

It is one of the nicest things about being a teacher to hear from the children when they have been out there in life for a while, sometimes years later, and to find out what has become of them—how they have found their place in life, what good fortune they have experienced, how they learned to bear sorrow. When these messages from the students make their way back into the school when the students are practically grown up, perhaps, and are firmly rooted in life, these are experiences that really give the teachers strength and reanimate them, even if they have been teaching for a long time.

If we make ourselves aware of everything that is working into the school at Eastertime, we get a feeling—and this is a feeling that you too should get, dear boys and girls—for what this time in school signifies in a whole human life between birth and death. It is a real summertime, life's sun time, and Easter in particular, as it is now starting to happen in nature, reminds us of it.

Then the teachers realize how happy they are to have the confidence of people like the parents who entrust their children to them. Because of all the effort they have made, the teachers are then really able to experience this: For years and years the parents have entrusted what is dearest to them to us in full confidence, and the school is fortunate in having been able to not only uphold this confidence but also to justify it, so that the parents can see their children leaving school, full of hope on entering life, with the same satisfaction that they had in trustingly sending them off to school for the first time.

All this is present in our hearts and souls at this time of year. I merely wanted to say a few words to impress it on the hearts and souls of the students and teachers.

All this will come about if something that must be present becomes a general practice among the students, namely love and devotion toward the faculty and devotion toward what you are learning through this school. If the right love prevails in the Waldorf School among parents, teachers, and students, then in what love can do when people are to be led through life by all that is beautiful and grand, this life will be able to prevail and to give people the forces they need.

This is why I have always asked you if you have succeeded in learning to really love your teachers. If you can learn to love them even more, it will be possible for everything to well up out of this love as if from a spring of fresh water. Then you will learn everything, and the Easter season will give you all it can. I would like to ask you, "Do you love your teachers?" [They all shout, "Yes!"] That is nice of you. Now, in this love that has developed between you, look at the ones who are now leaving school and resolve to follow them through life with your loving glances, and a wonderful relationship of love and friendship will be able to develop. And then the Waldorf School will be like a sun, able to ray out beautifully into life.

Address at the assembly at the beginning of the sixth school year

April 30, 1924

Dear children, dear boys and girls! To begin with, you will have to listen quietly for a little, because the first people I want to address are the parents who have joined us for this great celebration, both the ones who have brought very little children here to us and the ones who have accompanied their older children.

Dear parents of our students! We can certainly value and appreciate this moment in your emotional lives. Anyone who has already covered a good bit of distance in life, as is the case with parents, knows that life tests us with sorrows and joys, that it presents us with tests that bring joys as well as suffering. Your children are the most precious thing that life has given you. We who are running the Waldorf School know very well what it means to decide where to send your child to school. You do that under the influence of everything you have been through in your own life; you want your child to be able to go through life in the best way you know of.

It cannot be my task today to talk about how we try to introduce the children into life through an appropriate and humanly worthy form of instruction that takes all of life as its background. You can rest assured, however, that one result of our theory of education, our art of education, is that we know what it means that you as parents are sending your children to a particular school in order to set a lasting course for their lives, and we respect it. We have a sense of all-encompassing responsibility in taking the children out of the hands that have brought them here today, and we assure you that we really know what this means.

May we also find ways to come together in this feeling of responsibility, and may the occasion of today be repeated often. In the Waldorf School, in a school that is not yet acknowledged in broader circles, we need what we can gain from energetically working together with the parents, so I ask you to come to the school often for discussions and other purposes. What we and you want for the children will be best achieved if we can work effectively with the parents at home. We in the school will attempt to carry this out to the greatest extent possible.

Now I would like to turn to the children who are in school for the first time today. You need not understand much at all yet. What is happening today is something you already know something about, something you have already had to start learning. You have loved your parents; that is something you know how to do. Now you must also learn to love your teachers. If you love your teachers, you will be able to learn everything there is to learn, with a little help from them. This will happen very gently. You will have to learn to sit still for a while from time to time, but when the lesson is over you may run around outside again, but not too fast, so that you don't fall and hurt your head. You must also always be very friendly to each other. The main thing is to learn to sit still, to love your teachers, and to make sure that you and the others stay healthy.

Right at the beginning, as you were sitting here, from the lowest right up to the highest grades, you heard something very important from the dear lady who is the first grade teacher. You heard that these little folks have become something very different from what they were before. They have become schoolchildren. That is what she told you. You can become a schoolchild. But now, in order to connect the lowest and the highest grades, I would like to tell you that you can never leave school again.

You will leave the Waldorf School, to be sure. Some of you will leave after the eighth grade and some will leave after a few more grades. Just now we have had to send the first ones to complete the highest grade out into life. But when all that is over with, that is when you really start going to school, because the most important and meaningful school of all is the school of life, and you enter the school of life only when you have left school. It is our job to be the preparatory school for the school of life.

That is what your dear teachers are here for, and last of all I turn to them. When I look at the school like this, I have to say that the most important schoolchildren are the men and women who are the teachers! It is very important that they have come to this school, because they are learning all the time. And do you know from whom they want to learn the most? From you! They want to learn the best way for you to be able to bear sorrow and joy; they want to learn how it happens that you are healthy or sick. They have so much to learn from you so that out of the fullness of their love for you, they can teach you to be people who can stand on their own feet in life.

For this to happen, there is one thing that is more necessary than anything else. I always say this, but I would like to say it again because it cannot be said often enough. In the Waldorf School, the teachers take great inner pleasure in what they do. They know that they are working on life out there by working on what is most important in it—on the beginnings of life. When I see these happy faces on the first day of school, and among them the boys and girls who have been here longer and who have always answered me when I asked if you love your teachers—when I see you all like this, there is something I would also like to say to you today. During the vacation you were away from your teachers. Now that you are back in school things will go well only if you can again answer a certain question for me. Sometimes people forget things, but there is one thing you are not allowed to forget. You have planted love for your teachers in your souls. You have told me so again and again. Now that you have been out there for a while, I am going to ask you whether you have forgotten your love for your teachers during the vacation. If you have not forgotten, answer me with a good loud "No!" [The children shout, "No!] That is what will take you into the school year in the right way. Then you will pay attention and work hard, and everything will go well.

Dear students of the highest grade of all—that is, dear teachers! In this new school year, let us begin teaching with courage and enthusiasm to prepare these children for the school of life. Thus may the school be guided by the greatest leader of all, by the Christ Himself. May this be the case in our school. Let us go forward out of enthusiasm for what we have to do and out of love for the children; they are such a great joy to their teachers, and their teachers can help them learn so much. Let us continue our work with love and enthusiasm in the hearts of the children, with love and enthusiasm in the hearts of the teachers.

Onward, dear children and dear teachers, onward!

Lecture given at the fourth official meeting of the Independent Waldorf School Association: *How Teachers Interact with the Home in the Spirit of Waldorf Pedagogy*

June 1, 1924

Ladies and gentlemen! From the viewpoints the Waldorf School takes as its points of departure, there is not one path but many that lead away from the unnatural things that have been imposed on humanity, and especially on our public life, toward something natural that is being demanded by human nature in its broadest sense, so to speak. I intend to outline one such path, the path between the teacher and the parents' house, in the remarks I am going to present to you today.

You may say that this path can be taken for granted, and yet, ladies and gentlemen, not only has the path teachers and educators take to the parents' house been found to be very difficult at times, but there are many, many significant views on education that pay no attention to it at all. I need only remind you of something that was experienced as a great event in the course of German cultural development—the appearance of Johann Gottlieb Fichte in all fields. Today, however, we will only mention his appearance in the field of education. During one of the most difficult times in German history, he gave his penetrating "Speeches to the German Nation" in which he pointed out that healing and re-enlivening German life after the humiliation of 1806 would have to happen through education.[1] We can say that Johann Gottlieb Fichte, one of the noblest of all Germans, found the most beautiful and most significant words to say about education. However, he regarded it as a fundamental prerequisite for carrying out his pedagogical intentions that children be taken from their parents homes and cooped up together in special educational institutions that would be run according to strict principles and only by a unified state. After his time, we also witnessed a great variety of educational experiments in which children from certain circumstances were brought together in special places to be educated appropriately. In the course of humanity's evolution we

---

1. Johann Gottlieb Fichte, 1762–1814, *Reden an die deutsche Nation* ["Speeches to the German Nation"] given in Berlin during the Napoleonic occupation of 1807–08.

have seen numerous examples that necessitated the removal of children from their homes.

Although Waldorf education and its spirit work with at least as much urgency and at least as much out-of-the-depths of the human soul as the educational experiments sketched briefly above, this spirit of Waldorf education took a very different direction from the very beginning. It did not take superficialities as its starting point. It did not say that this or that social provision had to be made for the sake of the children. It did not say that children needed to be removed from their normal situations and placed in different ones. From the very beginning the spirit of Waldorf education was a purely pedagogical and methodological one. The social situation and the circumstances of the children's lives are accepted for what they are, and everything that is to be accomplished through Waldorf education is striven for on the basis of the inner spiritual foundations of pedagogy itself. We can thus say, in effect, that wherever educational difficulties arise because of a child's social situation or other circumstances, these are accepted as destiny by the spirit of Waldorf education, and methods are put into effect that will allow the difficulties to be overcome out of the spirit and out of teaching practices that are individualized for the child in question to the greatest possible extent. This means, however, that a school like the Waldorf School stands in the midst of actual life. In actual life, if we are dealing with a school that takes children at age six or seven, they are coming from home, and since we have no boarding facility they remain at home and in the care of their parents during the time when they are not in school. Thus the entire thrust of education in the Waldorf School is to work together with the parents. In particular, as we shall see, we must feel, sense, and think together with the parents.

No doubt many of you have often been presented with the idea of the significance of the stages of life for the life of a child.

There are two or three of life's stages that are of concern to our theory of education. The first begins at birth and ends at the change of teeth, the second begins at the change of teeth and ends at puberty, and the third continues from there until approximately the twenty-first year of life. If we have an unprejudiced sense of how things are, each of these stages in the life of a child shows us the child in a totally different constitution of soul and of body. Let us first consider the child's soul constitution.

Until the change of teeth, the child is definitely dependent on imitation for learning what is taught. What you demonstrate to the child works like an outer stimulus that calls upon the child's entire bodily organization—in some places more visibly, in others less visibly—to imitate the impression. To substantiate this, we need only keep in mind the decisive fact that children acquire their native language wholly through imitation, which works deeply into the organization of their bodies and souls. We must take into account that the vibration, the waves of movement, of any spoken sound is experienced much more intensely in childhood than it is later on in life. Even in speaking, when it is a person's native language that is in question, any adjusting of the larynx, any inner ensouling of the organs, is based on imitation. This is how it is with everything in the child's life until the change of teeth.

Nowadays, when a misunderstanding, or rather numerous misunderstandings, generate great errors in our otherwise so admirable scientific world-view, we often talk about the hereditary basis of one or the other thing a child acquires in the first stage of life up to the change of teeth. But as far as the child is concerned, the only basis for this talk of heredity is the fact that the people who are talking about it have no real sense of observation. Otherwise they would find out that basically much of what we attribute today to this dark and mysterious heredity must actually be looked for in the child's clearly comprehensible tendency to imitate.

However, consider how close the child's soul life, which arises out of this imitative activity, is to the life of the parents simply because the child is a being who imitates. If we really grasp how strong the tendency toward imitation is in the child, we come to have a holy awe and a profound respect for the child/parent relationship. And if we then look at the basis for all this in spiritual cosmic connections, then we are truly able to say that since a human being is a spiritual being prior to embarking on a physical existence, this person—in spite of being a free being—enters earthly existence with a very specific destiny with regard to the forms, if not the routines, of life. If we look on the one hand at how this destiny unrolls with an inner regularity from the smallest experiences of childhood to a ripe old age, and on the other hand at how the child grows close to the parents by being an imitative being, if we really see all this in the context of all the underlying spiritual connections, we begin to have sensations that are religious in character, you might say, about what is given to us as teachers and educators when a child is entrusted to us. And these almost religious sensations make us strongly inclined to want to understand, when a child is entrusted to us on entering school, precisely how this child is connected to his or her parents.

It may be said that theoretical pedagogical considerations or abstract principles are truly not what determine how the spirit of Waldorf education sets out to meet the parents of the children. Rather, it is something living, just as everything else in the Waldorf school is meant to be something living. It is a living thing; it is the Waldorf teacher's active need to be able not only to approach the child in spirit but also to find a way from the child to the parents through every expression of soul the child presents, through every motivating force, through every type of childish impulsiveness, and even through every gesture and every hand movement. This confirms our understanding of the child, which we Waldorf teachers need above all else if we are to teach by deriving our educational impulses from the very nature of the child in question. First and foremost, we can confirm that we are looking at a child in the right way by turning to the parents standing behind him or her. This is the case even when the parent/child relationship is not absolutely harmonious. In actual life what grows out of children and parents living together can manifest in the greatest possible variety of ways. Of course we have an inner feeling of happiness when we look at the destiny of a child who has the possibility of living in fully harmonious circumstances with exemplary parents. But may we not pose a counterquestion to this? If we observe life, either contemporary or historical life, without bias, do we not find that the greatest spirits, not only intellectual geniuses but also geniuses of virtue and moral action, have often sprung from grave disharmonies between child and parents? Waldorf teachers must acquire the habit of not criticizing the child/parent relationship, but of accepting it objectively, because their acquaintance with the parents can shed light on the child's idiosyncrasies.

Thus it is not some pedagogical principle that challenges the Waldorf teacher to find a way to get to know the parents, but rather an inner heartfelt need, just as Waldorf education in general is essentially a pedagogy of the heart.

Let us now look at something else, namely the fact that teachers are now obliged to take on part of what used to be provided solely by the parents of children of elementary-school age. On entering elementary school, a child is going through the change of teeth. Nowadays children are sent to school somewhat too early; elementary-school age actually only begins with the change of teeth, but that is not the main point here.

When a child is sent to school and entrusted to a teacher, the teacher must take on a part of education or child-rearing that acquires its specific character from the fact that the child's entire soul life, the child's entire constitution of soul and spirit, is also transformed at the change of teeth. After that, the child is no longer an imitative being, although the principle of imitation does persist for several years into the child's time in elementary school. Fundamentally, however, the child is now no longer an imitative being, but a being who is stimulated by what it meets in the form of images, through our structuring what we present in an appropriate and artistic way, you might say. At this age, children no longer tend to apply themselves imitatively and with their entire constitution to what is presented to them. Instead, they shift to the principle of natural authority. Whereas earlier it was the children's will that imitatively traced what was demonstrated to them in their entire constitution, now it is their feeling that likes or dislikes what their teacher presents to them in images, including the images of his or her entire personality and actions, of the composition of his or her speech, and so forth. And the authority that prevails in school between the change of teeth and puberty must not be arbitrarily imposed. It must be a matter of course.

Without admitting this, it is impossible to look at how human life unfolds as a whole. It is so easy to say that we should always use visual aids in our lessons. I do not mean to say anything against visual aids, but they should not become a means of trivializing instruction. We cannot take it as a principle to reduce everything to the level the children are already on. The point is that only those things that directly nurture the children through visualization need to be cloaked in a visual representation. But take a circumstance from religious or moral life—how are we supposed to use visual aids in this case? Aside from that, however, the inner soul nature of the children is such that something is true because a teacher to whom they feel sympathetic, who is an authority to them as a matter of course, has pronounced it true. They feel something to be beautiful because a natural authority finds it beautiful; they find something good because this authority finds it good. The authority figure incorporates the true, the beautiful and the good. It is bad for a person to have to acquire a feeling for the true, the good, and the beautiful as a matter of principle, on the basis of abstract commandments or all kinds of rational rules, before having acquired it at the right age—the age between the change of teeth and puberty—by having it confront him or her in the person of another human being. We should first learn that something is true because a respected person declares it true, and only later recognize the inner abstract laws of truth, which actually can have an effect on us only after we achieve sexual maturity.

Surely you do not expect someone who wrote *The Philosophy of Freedom* over thirty years ago to go to bat for the principle of authority in a place where it does not belong. However, the authoritative principle that children demand by their very nature absolutely does belong in the elementary school. Teachers themselves, with their rationality, their hearts and feelings, and their whole nature as human beings, are guidelines with regard to the true, the good, and the beautiful as the children are meant to embrace them. The human relationship that comes about reaches right into how the children construe the true, the good, and the beautiful. All this is presented in greater detail in various pedagogical writings on Waldorf education which are available for you to read.[2]

---

2. See Rudolf Steiner's *The Renewal of Education*, Kolisko Archive Publications for Rudolf Steiner Schools Fellowship Publications, Forest Row, Sussex, England, 1980 [*Die Erneuerung der pädagogisch-didaktischen Kunst durch Geisteswissenschaft*, Dornach, 1977], 14 lectures given in Basel, 1920, GA 301;

But let us now consider the position Waldorf teachers are in as a result of acknowledging this principle of natural authority and trying to apply it to its fullest extent. They depend on not having this natural authority undermined in any way. We must keep in mind that at the age when the change of teeth is taking place, even in families in which a lack of harmony prevails between the child and the parents, the child is inwardly close to the parents. This closeness is so strong that it basically outshines anything else that comes under consideration with regard to the being of the child at this age. This means that even if a child confronts his or her parents with antipathy, to use a severe term, a totally unshakable authoritative relationship to the parents is present subconsciously. I can present this only briefly here, but the matter can be verified in all its details. A true psychology, a true study of the soul, teaches us that even when children come into conflict with their parents and home when they are losing their baby teeth or in the years just after that, they are actually totally under the authority of the parents in the subtle, subconscious psychological layers of their being. And who would wish it otherwise? This is simply the relationship nature provides. If I were to depict the course that humanity's evolution would

---

2. (continued) *Education and Modern Spiritual Life,* Garber Publications, Blauvelt, NY, 1989 [*Gegenwärtiges Geistesleben und Erziehung,* Dornach, 1923], 14 lectures given in Ilkley, 1923, GA 307; *The Roots of Education,* Anthroposophic Press, Hudson, NY, 1996 [*Anthroposophische Pädagogik und ihre Voraussetzungen,* Dornach, 1972], 5 lectures given in Bern, 1924, GA 309; *Human Values in Education,* Rudolf Steiner Press, London, 1971 [*Der pädagogische Wert der Menschenerkenntnis und der Kulturwert der Pädagogik,* Dornach 1965], 10 lectures given in Arnheim, 1924, GA 310; *The Kingdom of Childhood,* Anthroposophic Press, Hudson, NY, 1995 [*Die Kunst des Erziehens aus dem Erfassen der Menschenwesenheit,* Dornach, 1979], 7 lectures given in Torquay, 1924, GA 311; *The Education of the Child and Early Lectures on Education,* Anthroposophic Press, Hudson, NY, 1996 [*Die Erziehung des Kindes vom Gesichtspunkte der Geisteswissenschaft,* Dornach, 1978].

follow if this were not the case, it would make a horrible picture. This means, however, that in their now completely different field of activity, where teachers are no longer examples to imitate but speakers who use their authority to present what enters the child, teachers must take a more subtle approach in influencing what the child has become in his or her inmost being as a result of parents and home. There is no other way of responding to the individuality of a child with your authority than by being able to link up fully consciously with what the child has become as a result of parents and home. The instinctive result of this in the Waldorf teacher is an inner urge to establish a connection to the parents.

There is a very specific reason why this urge develops. The spirit of Waldorf education is not a one-sided one; it encompasses the spirit, the soul, and the body equally. It would be a total misunderstanding of the spirit of Waldorf Education to believe that the physical aspect, whether in a healthy or an unhealthy state, is in any way underestimated in comparison to the spiritual aspect. The spirit of Waldorf education takes into account the whole human being in a child. But because it takes the whole human being into account without actually having the whole human being—it only has the child during school hours and perhaps for a short time before and after—it must experience an inner need to be in the closest possible contact with the parents, with the home in which the child spends the rest of his or her time.

It really is true with us—and I have often said this, particularly within the Waldorf School itself—that an educator does not need to be afraid of large classes. To set up small classes for pedagogical reasons means to count on a pedagogical weakness. That is not what is going on here. If it were desirable to work toward having smaller classes in the Waldorf school, the reason for it would be so that the teacher would have more possibility of establishing a connection to the parents of all the students in the class. That is what the teacher must do, out of the whole spirit of the Waldorf school.

But let us consider something else, since I am only trying to highlight a few of life's stages. Those who can observe children in real life find that there is an extremely important point in life between the ages of nine and ten, approximately. You can see this point approaching; a certain inner crisis makes its presence known. It is not that the children start asking especially rational questions, but this crisis becomes evident when otherwise lively children start to hang their heads, when quiet ones become loud, when they give evidence of all sorts of unhealthy conditions, and so on. What is going on here is that in the child's subconscious—and a great deal in the being of a child is in the subconscious rather than in consciousness—a question appears, a question that is not formulated rationally, but is active only in perception: Is the natural authority that has given me what is true, good, and beautiful up to now, is the natural authority that is the personification of truth, goodness and beauty, actually that? The doubt need not be expressed out loud, but it is there; it infuses the life of the child in the way I have described.

At this stage in a child's life, it is important for the teacher to have a healthy, independent gift of observation in order to find the right word and the right way of acting. Many things are needed—tact, instinct, intuition. Then you will be able to do something at this point in the child's life that will be of wide-ranging significance for the entire earthly life that follows. If you find the comments, the actions and the relationship that can confirm for the child in an individually appropriate way that he or she was right in seeing a natural authority in you, then you have done something out of your inmost soul to become a true benefactor of that child.

Lucky the person who after this point around the ninth or tenth year can continue to look up to and respect an authority as a matter of course! No individual can become a free being in the course of his or her life without first learning, before entering puberty, to arrange life in accordance with how a highly respected person acts. To submit out of inner instinctive freedom in this way, to face such a person, recognizing that it is right to do as he or she does—that is what starts to make something out of the potentials for freedom that are concealed in a person.

In short, we as Waldorf teachers must maintain our natural authority in all respects and in the most subtle way. How can we do this? It is possible if our interaction with parents arouses the feeling in them that it is all right for them to influence their children to see the natural authority in the teacher. This may sound trivial, but it is true: Waldorf teachers should never pass up the opportunity to show themselves to the children's parents in their true colors, so that the parents know who they are dealing with. This can sometimes be done in five minutes. The parent's tone of voice, the nuance of each sentence they speak about the school, should be directed toward supporting natural authority in school. The connection between school and home cannot be close enough.

Still a third thing: If you have in front of you two, three or four sets of curricula and school regulations, all of them very cleverly thought out, then you know what you have to do. You have the curriculum, you have the regulations; that is what you have to do. But that is not how things are in the Waldorf School. If we are thinking in the spirit of the Waldorf School, it is right to think that some things must be different than they are in public education. Many people today cannot grasp that. And cleverness is so prevalent in our times. I cannot emphasize enough how clever people in our times are in comparison to other times. But it is just this rational cleverness—and I mean this quite seriously;

I am not being ironic—that commits the greatest stupidities. Nevertheless, people are clever, and this is expressed in a great variety of ways. If thirty people sit together and plan a school reform, it can be so clever that it cannot be disputed. And then lay thinkers can say, "That's brilliant, it would be impossible to create better schools than these people have done with their points 1, 2, 3, and 4." But just try to take it further, and look at the schools that have been created through those points 1, 2, 3, and 4. The principles are very clever, the statutes and paragraphs are very clever, but you cannot do anything with them in real life. The only way to do anything in real life is to feel life itself pulsing within you and to create out of this pulsing life.

This is where Waldorf teachers stand: They have no statutes and paragraphs, but only advice and suggestions which they must shape according to their own individualities. If you prescribe strictly what teachers have to do in school, then they should all be just alike. Just think of the consequences of that. If the regulations were seriously enforced, if we were to put into effect these very well-meaning abstract pedagogical principles that hold that there is only one way of teaching, then you would no longer be able to tell one teacher from another. You would meet one teacher and think it was some other one, because they would both be teaching according to the same abstract principles. But teachers are human beings. They are individuals. And they can only work if they can put themselves into it with the full independence of their being. Only then can they be really effective. But then they have to know life. You can only work in real live if you allow life to affect you. But what kind of life do you encounter in school? The parents' life as it continues to work in the children. Our teachers are steered away from paragraphs and principles toward the real, immediate life of the children. This must flow into our methodology, into how we arrange all of our teaching.

So, ladies and gentlemen, if you could be a fly on the wall and listen in on our teachers' meetings sometimes, you would hear how all the details of home are actually being taken into account and how intimately they are discussed with regard to how they shed light on the children. And if you were that fly on the wall, you would also find out that these teachers' meetings are an ongoing learning process, that our educational practices are constantly evolving toward higher and more subtle effectiveness. It cannot be different if the school is meant to be a living organism, rather than a dead one. This means that the Waldorf School, because it calls itself an independent school, is an institution whose innermost being points to parents and home with regard to understanding the child as a total being.

Let us say that we get to know a child who is lacking in intellectual ability. That can happen. And there are many ways in which a lack of intellectual ability can be corrected, can be developed into something better. But we need a point of departure. Let us say that we get to know the child's father and mother, and they are very intelligent. It does sometimes happen that children who are not intellectually gifted have very intelligent parents. It can also be just the opposite, that parents who are not intellectually gifted have highly gifted children. In any case, we will learn a very great deal about alleviating the child's lack of intellectual ability if we look at the parents whom the child imitated up to the change of teeth. If we do so, we will find not only a theoretical explanation, but also suggestions for implementing what we have to do about it. The emotional life plays a very significant role in children of school age. It even plays into morality in that it receives the good only through sympathy for the good in the teacher. Children's emotional life becomes transparent when we can see through their feeling into their parents' particular variety of feeling life. This applies equally to the life of the will.

People whose intelligence tells them that an individual must be like this and such because that is average and proper human nature need not consider the parents. However, if we know that things and beings have origins, if we look to the source rather than to something abstract, then we must consider the child's parents and home.

Waldorf education leads us along the path toward reality because it tries to live and breathe the spirit of reality, a spirit that is in accordance with nature and in accordance with the soul. And this path toward reality leads away from school and toward the parents' home. This is the reason behind everything that can awaken the teacher's interest in the parents and the parents' interest in the teachers in the school. The parents' evenings that are organized by the Waldorf School are there in order to create a bond between school and home. What we do in these parents' evenings is meant to allow the parents to see the attitude and soul-constitution of the faculty.

This, ladies and gentlemen, is the practical implementation of what is ultimately present as the highest—I cannot say principle, but the highest view in the spirit of Waldorf education. Out of the depths of their inner soul life and out of this spirit of Waldorf education, Waldorf teachers must realize that the parents are entrusting the school with the most precious thing they have when they send their children to us. These parents have had many experiences in life; perhaps they have been tested by life. This does not mean that they wish their children to remain untested, but they do wish them to be spared some of the difficult experiences that they themselves had to go through. For this and many other reasons, parents attach a great deal of hope to the moment when they entrust their child to a school. Out of the whole spirit of Waldorf education, our teachers know what is being entrusted to them. On the basis of views such as those I have characterized, they would like their effect on the children to be such that when the children are released from school and return to their parents, the parents can say, "We knew it all the time, ever since we first saw the school, that our hopes would be fulfilled." However, this is not a conclusion they can come to at the last minute when their children graduate. It can mature gradually only through the interaction between school and home.

Thus, we can turn our backs on many different educational experiments, and even on well-intentioned pedagogical ideals, and turn to the spirit of Waldorf education, realizing that there is an extremely healthy instinct at work in children being together with their parents, and that it must therefore also be healthy for the school to grow close to this relationship by finding the right way to approach the parents.

Among the many things that the Waldorf School aspires to, which can all be characterized by saying that this school wants to rise above abstract principles and cleverness to a reality that is full of life, the main thing is that the Waldorf School wants to find a way to the most life-filled reality in the child's existence. And in the existence of the small child, the child of school age, this reality is the parents.

This school with its spirit wants to be, not a school of theories, abstractions, and inflexible theoretical principles, but one full of life and reality. That is why it tries to find its way into the reality of the parents' home.

1 9 2 5

*Rudolf Steiner's Last Words to the Faculty and Students
of the Free Waldorf School in Stuttgart[1]*

Goetheanum, March 15, 1925

My Dear Faculty of the Free Waldorf School!

It is a great privation to me not to be among you. I must now leave important decisions in your hands—decisions in which, since the School was founded, I have naturally taken part. This is a time of being tested by fate. I am with you with my thoughts. If I am not to risk endlessly extending the time of my physical impediment I cannot do more than that now.

> May the reality of thoughts unite us
> Since we must be separated in space.—
> May what we have already completed together
> Now work through the company of teachers.
> May it ripple through your own thoughts
> For thoughts that want to come to much
> Do not have their wings free.

Therefore, so long as nothing else is possible, we must work toward unity of spirit ever more intensely. The Waldorf School is truly a problem child, but above all it is also a true sign of the fruitfulness of Anthroposophy within the spiritual life of humanity.

---

1. From *Die Konstitution der Allgemeinen Anthroposophischen Gesellschaft under der Freien Hochschule für Geisteswissenschaft. Der Wiederaufbau des Goetheanum 1924/1925* (GA260a) pp. 405–6.

If the faculty truly carries in its heart the consciousness of this fruitfulness then the good spirits who reign over the School will be able to be effective, and divine spiritual power will reign in the deeds of the teachers.

Out of such reflections I would send you all my dearest thoughts and greetings.

I shall still send a brief note to the students that I would ask you to read in class.

Most Cordially,

Rudolf Steiner

. . . .

Goetheanum, March 15, 1925

To my dear students—girls and boys—of the Waldorf School!

To my great sorrow I have not been able to be with you for a long time now. And yet it would give me the greatest satisfaction if I could spend some time with my beloved girls and boys. But, as long as I cannot do so, I shall send you many heartfelt and good thoughts.

You have given me truly great pleasure in sending me your work. Thank you very much.

I hope I can appear among you again soon.

To all, a cordial greeting

Rudolf Steiner

THE FOUNDATIONS
OF WALDORF EDUCATION

THE FIRST FREE WALDORF SCHOOL opened its doors in Stuttgart, Germany, in September, 1919, under the auspices of Emil Molt, the Director of the Waldorf Astoria Cigarette Company and a student of Rudolf Steiner's spiritual science and particularly of Steiner's call for social renewal.

It was only the previous year—amid the social chaos following the end of World War I—that Emil Molt, responding to Steiner's prognosis that truly human change would not be possible unless a sufficient number of people received an education that developed the whole human being, decided to create a school for his workers' children. Conversations with the Minister of Education and with Rudolf Steiner, in early 1919, then led rapidly to the forming of the first school.

Since that time, more than six hundred schools have opened around the globe—from Italy, France, Portugal, Spain, Holland, Belgium, Great Britain, Norway, Finland and Sweden to Russia, Georgia, Poland, Hungary, Rumania, Israel, South Africa, Australia, Brazil, Chile, Peru, Argentina, Japan etc.—making the Waldorf School Movement the largest independent school movement in the world. The United States, Canada, and Mexico alone now have more than 120 schools.

Although each Waldorf school is independent, and although there is a healthy oral tradition going back to the first Waldorf teachers and to Steiner himself, as well as a growing body of secondary literature, the true foundations of the Waldorf method and spirit remain the many lectures that Rudolf Steiner gave on the subject. For five years (1919–24), Rudolf Steiner, while simultaneously working on many other fronts, tirelessly dedicated himself to the dissemination of the idea of Waldorf education. He gave manifold lectures to teachers, parents, the general public, and even the children themselves. New schools were founded. The Movement grew.

While many of Steiner's foundational lectures have been translated and published in the past, some have never appeared in English, and many have been virtually unobtainable for years. To remedy this situation and to establish a coherent basis for Waldorf Education, Anthroposophic Press has decided to publish the complete series of Steiner lectures and writings on education in a uniform series. This series will thus constitute an authoritative foundation for work in educational renewal, for Waldorf teachers, parents, and educators generally.

RUDOLF STEINER'S LECTURES
(AND WRITINGS) ON EDUCATION

I. *Allgemeine Menschenkunde als Grundlage der Pädagogik. Pedagogischer Grundkurs,* 14 Lectures, Stuttgart, 1919 (GA293). Previously *Study of Man.* **Foundations of Human Experience** (Anthroposophic Press, 1996).

II. *Erziehungskunst Methodisch-Didaktisches,* 14 Lectures, Stuttgart, 1919 (GA294). **Practical Advice to Teachers** (Rudolf Steiner Press, 1976).

III. *Erziehungskunst. Methodisch-Didaktisches,* 15 Discussions, Stuttgart, 1919 (GA 295). **Discussions with Teachers** (Anthroposophic Press, 1996).

IV. *Die Erziehungsfrage als soziale Frage,* 6 Lectures, Dornach, 1919 (GA296). **Education as a Social Problem** (Anthroposophic Press, 1969).

V. *Die Waldorf Schule und ihr Geist,* 6 Lectures, Stuttgart and Basel, 1919 (GA 297). **The Spirit of the Waldorf School** (Anthroposophic Press, 1995).

VI. *Rudolf Steiner in der Waldorfschule, Vorträge und Ansprachen,* Stuttgart, 1919–1924 (GA 298). **Rudolf Steiner in the Waldorf School—Lectures and Conversations**, Anthroposophic Press, 1996.

VII. *Geisteswissenschaftliche Sprachbetrachtungen,* 6 Lectures, Stuttgart, 1919 (GA 299). **The Genius of Language** (Anthroposophic Press, 1995).

VIII. *Konferenzen mit den Lehren der Freien Waldorfschule 1919–1924,* 3 Volumes (GA 300). **Conferences with Teachers** (Steiner Schools Fellowship, 1986, 1987, 1988, 1989).

IX. *Die Erneuerung der Pädagogisch-didaktischen Kunst durch Geisteswissenschaft,* 14 Lectures, Basel, 1920 (GA 301). **The Renewal of Education** (Kolisko Archive Publications for Steiner Schools Fellowship Publications, Michael Hall, Forest Row, East Sussex, UK, 1981).

X. *Menschenerkenntnis und Unterrichtsgestaltung,* 8 Lectures, Stuttgart, 1921 (GA 302). Previously *The Supplementary Course—Upper School* and *Waldorf Education for Adolescence.* **High School Education** (Anthroposophic Press, 1996).

XI. *Erziehung und Unterrricht aus Menschenerkenntnis,* 9 Lectures, Stuttgart, 1920, 1922, 1923 (GA302a). The first four lectures available as **Balance in Teaching** (Mercury Press, 1982); last three lectures as **Deeper Insights into Education** (Anthroposophic Press, 1988).

XII. *Die Gesunde Entwickelung des Menschenwesens,* 16 Lectures, Dornach, 1921–22 (GA303). **Soul Economy and Waldorf Education** (Anthroposophic Press, 1986).

XIII. *Erziehungs- und Unterrichtsmethoden auf anthroposophischer Grundlage,* 9 Public lectures, various cities, 1921–22 (GA304). **Waldorf Education and Anthroposophy I** (Anthroposophic Press, 1995).

XIV. *Anthroposophische Menschenkunde und Pädagogik,* 9 Public lectures, various cities, 1923–24 (GA304a). **Waldorf Education and Anthroposophy II** (Anthroposophic Press, 1996).

XV. *Die geistig-seelischen Grundkräfte der Erziehungskunst,* 12 Lectures, 1 Special Lecture, Oxford 1922 (GA 305). **The Spiritual Ground of Education** (Garber Publications, n.d.).

XVI. *Die pädagogische Praxis vom Gesichtspunkte geisteswissenschaftlicher Menschenerkenntnis,* 8 Lectures, Dornach, 1923 (GA306). **The Child's Changing Consciousness and Waldorf Education** (Anthroposophic Press, 1996).

XVII. *Gegenwärtiges Geistesleben und Erziehung,* 14 Lectures, Ilkley, 1923 (GA307). **A Modern Art of Education** (Rudolf Steiner Press, 1981) and **Education and Modern Spiritual Life** (Garber Publications, 1989).

XVIII. *Die Methodik des Lehrens und die Lebensbedingungen des Erziehens,* 5 Lectures, Stuttgart, 1924 (GA308). **The Essentials of Education** (Rudolf Steiner Press, 1968).

XIX. *Anthroposophische Pädagogik und ihre Voraussetzungen,* 5 Lectures, Bern, 1924 (GA 309). **The Roots of Education** (Anthroposophic Press, 1996).

XX. *Der pädagogische Wert der Menschenerkenntnis und der Kulturwert der Pädagogik,* 10 Public lectures, Arnheim, 1924 (GA310). **Human Values in Education** (Rudolf Steiner Press, 1971).

XXI. *Die Kunst des Erziehens aus dem Erfassen der Menschenwesenheit,* 7 Lectures, Torquay, 1924 (GA311). **The Kingdom of Childhood** (Anthroposophic Press, 1995).

XXII. *Geisteswissenschaftliche Impulse zur Entwicklung der Physik. Erster naturwissenschaftliche Kurs: Licht, Farbe, Ton—Masse, Elektrizität, Magnetismus,* 10 Lectures, Stuttgart, 1919–20 (GA 320). **The Light Course** (Steiner Schools Fellowship,1977).

XXIII. *Geisteswissenschaftliche Impulse zur Entwickelung der Physik. Zweiter naturwissenschaftliche Kurs: die Wärme auf die Grenze positiver und negativer Materialität,*14 Lectures, Stuttgart, 1920 (GA 321). **The Warmth Course** (Mercury Press, 1988).

XXIV. *Das Verhältnis der verschiedenen naturwissenschaftlichen Gebiete zur Astronomie. Dritter naturwissenschaftliche Kurs: Himmelskunde in Bezeiehung zum Menschen und zur Menschenkunde,* 18 Lectures, Stuttgart, 1921 (GA 323). Available in typescript only as "**The Relation of the Diverse Branches of Natural Science to Astronomy.**"

XXV. Miscellaneous.

INDEX

Dᴜʀɪɴɢ ᴛʜᴇ ʟᴀsᴛ ᴛᴡᴏ ᴅᴇᴄᴀᴅᴇs of the nineteenth century the Austrian-born Rudolf Steiner (1861–1925) became a respected and well-published scientific, literary, and philosophical scholar, particularly known for his work on Goethe's scientific writings. After the turn of the century he began to develop his earlier philosophical principles into an approach to methodical research of psychological and spiritual phenomena.

His multifaceted genius has led to innovative and holistic approaches in medicine, science, education (Waldorf schools), special education, philosophy, religion, economics, agriculture (Biodynamic method), architecture, drama, new arts of eurythmy and speech, and other fields. In 1924 he founded the General Anthroposophical Society, which today has branches throughout the world.